D1492013

Letters from a Soldier

Letters from a Soldier

❧

WALTER ROBSON

with an introduction by
HENRY WILLIAMSON

FABER AND FABER
24 Russell Square
London

First published in mcmlx
by Faber and Faber Limited
24 Russell Square London W.C.1
Printed in Great Britain by
Latimer Trend & Co Ltd Plymouth

CONTENTS

7

INTRODUCTION

Before anything is said about this remarkable and moving collection of letters written by a soldier from the field to his wife in England during 1943, 1944, and 1945, I feel I should say that, in my view, books about war can be put, roughly, into three categories.

First, those written by angry or disturbed, one might almost say ill-based young men whose unhappy experiences in childhood are projected with magnification into later war-memories which they were unable to face with the ordinary man's sense of sharingness in comradeship—so much in the books of these authors is described in blackest colours of doom without relief, with savagery, satire, and often falsification.

The 1914–18 war produced many such books, the most widely read of which was *All Quiet on the Western Front*, which had the tension of imagined dread, a feeling always more terrible than action itself, of one who had not gone through a battle; and of which the worst was *Generals Die in Bed*, a libellous work of no merit and again, giving the impression of inexperience, and incidentally of lonely soldiering.

Second, sober books of fact, which are not generally read by the great public, despite their considerable merit. Lt.-Colonel Rowland Feilding's *War Letters to a Wife* was one

9

of the very best in this class, dealing with the First World War. It is direct, fully descriptive, and avoids no aspect of the beastliness and pity of war—although always recorded with simplicity. It leaves nothing out, but puts in nothing afterwards. Mr. Stephen Graham's *A Private in the Guards* is another excellent book, based soberly on personal experience, the work of a trained writer (and soldier) which also should be republished, because it contains, with Lt.-Colonel Feilding's *War Letters*, data of historical interest.

In a slightly different vein in this second category is Mr. Edmund Blunden's *Undertones of War*, also a personal work but generally speaking it has less 'hard news'. Even so, it is a genuine record of a poet whose courage was spiritual rather than physical—if the two can, indeed, be separated. Among the poets, we have Wilfred Owen's *Poems*, published posthumously with a brief Introduction by his friend, Mr. Siegfried Sassoon, whose own poems of actual battle and camp scenes (if one may exclude the satirical verse, except as evidence of the line soldier's genuine bitterness in those days of almost complete separation between the 'gilded Staff' who ordered from afar, and the men who held and tried to push forward the line against an enemy as resolute and courageous as themselves) are masterly, that is, true in spirit and letter.

Third, the War Histories. These are compiled from innumerable sources when the battlefields are silent, save for the twitter of finches among the seeding flowers of the waste land, and the occasional roaring shudder of piles of 'dud' shells and grenades, after collection by labourers, usually displaced persons. I watched some of these rusty heaps being detonated, each of several hundred tons' weight, in The Labyrinthe, and at Beaumont Hamel, Thiepval, Verdun, and other places where men had died in their thousands as attack and counter-attack 'dunged with rotten death' the soil of France and Flanders during the months and years when the Western Front was seen from aircraft at night as a great livid wound extending from the sandhills adjoining the North Sea to the forests lying below the Swiss Alps.

Standing in a class by itself is perhaps the best all-round book on the 1914–18 war, being Sir Winston Spencer Churchill's *The World Crisis*. This autobiographical work contains some of the finest descriptions of the effects of actual warfare in any language. And not far from that classic personal-historic work is *War Letters of General Monash*, an Australian; Lt.-General Sir John Monash was a civilian when war broke out in 1914, and a Corps commander in 1918, and was perhaps the most brilliant military brain revealed by that war. His literary gifts match his powers of organization.

Then there are the novels written after the war, among the best being *Way of Revelation*, by Wilfrid Ewart, a captain of the Scots Guard; and *Winged Victory*, by Victor Yeates, a Camel pilot on the Western Front. *Way of Revelation*, alas, suffers from the sad fact that its climax (a scene at the Albert Hall Victory Ball in 1919) was altered by the hand of a lady novelist; and on reading the galley proofs of his novel, Ewart, a young man who had been badly shaken in the battles of 1915, 1916, and 1918, had a stroke, leaving him with partial loss of speech. He died a few months later, accidentally shot in Mexico City by a stray revolver bullet fired by a reveller in the streets below, which struck the head of Ewart watching from an hotel balcony. One hopes that somewhere the original ending to his novel is preserved, for Wilfrid Ewart was a great novelist in the classic tradition.

Coming now, across the years, to the present collection of *Letters from a Soldier*, it takes its place beside James Farrar's *The Unreturning Spring*, a brilliant and courageous record by a boy of genius, who was killed in the R.A.F. at the age of 20 years, in 1944. It is a remarkable collection, the more so because the letters reveal the personality of the writer to be a man as self-less and noble as any met with through the medium of print.

'Robbie', the writer of the letters, was 6350810 Lance-Corporal Walter Stanley Robson, stretcher bearer in the 1st Battalion The Queen's Royal West Kent Regiment. He married 'Margaret Gunn' less than two months before he was sent abroad. He was, in his wife's words:

'. . . the eldest of eight children of a working-class family and his formal schooling was at an elementary school and ended at fourteen . . . always he set himself a very high standard of integrity and behaviour. Politically he was to the left, but highly idealistic and had perhaps more in common with the ideas of Brotherhood of the early Christian community. Almost our whole marriage was contained in our letters. All the differences that have to be ironed out and the adjustments that have to be made when two people decide to share their lives had to be carried out in this cumbersome and uncertain way . . . it may be that some expression of apprehension that Robbie may have shown refers to some previous letter or discussion which does not appear now in the book. Or it may be that he was expecting me to disagree about something he had done or said; or that he feared to fall behind the standard he had set himself.'

Not all the letters Robbie wrote to 'Margaret Gunn' are included here, as they were of a personal nature; but the collection now published surely speaks for itself.

One would mention only two incidents, which to an old soldier, with a respect for his opposite number, are most moving. There is the happening, during the days and nights of continuous fighting in the Italian mountains, when the stretcher bearers in Robbie's squad, coming off duty, stumble into the aid post and seeing the photograph of 'Margaret Gunn' pinned on the wall, go to it and kiss it, surely a symbol of the highest spiritual love; for in those moments all that Britain meant to them, in the truth of spirit, was in a woman's portrait.

There is the other occasion, when two of the stretcher bearers, Tony and Percy, returning to their bandaged wounded in a certain house found the Germans in occupation, and 'got on famously' with them. 'They were smashing blokes, and two helped them back with the wounded. They passed Hermy and I who were having a long job with a broken pelvis. It was in Jerry's power to take them both prisoners, he didn't . . . wish they hadn't been such smashing blokes.'

In the First World War, the most highly decorated non-commissioned soldier in the British Army was also a lance-corporal and stretcher bearer. He was William Coltman of the North Staffordshire Regiment. He was awarded the Victoria Cross; the Distinguished Conduct Medal, with bar; and the Military Medal, with bar. Such honours were deserved; but one might say, also, that a stretcher bearer was a freer man than the ordinary foot-soldier, in that he could say with Wilfred Owen, in that dead soldier's immortal verse:

> *I, too, have dropped off fear—*
>   *Behind the barrage, dead as my platoon,*

And sailed my spirit surging, light and clear
Past the entanglement where hopes lay strewn;

I have made fellowships—
Untold of happy lovers in old song.
For love is not the binding of fair lips
With the soft silk of eyes that look and long,

By Joy, whose ribbon slips,—
But wound with war's hard wire whose stakes are
strong;
Bound with the bandage of the arm that drips;
Knit in the welding of the rifle-thong.

In this book, too, is the saving grace of humour, by which tensions, unbearable by the solitary soldier if he be apart from his fellows in spirit (apart from his father in love as a child?) are released. The cartoons of Bruce Bairnsfather, in the Great War, were of great help to many of us then. In his fine book, *The Anatomy of Courage*, written by Lord Moran when he was a battalion doctor in those days, it is said that 'courage is expendable'. Lance-Corporal Robson did not save any of his courage for himself. He survived the war; but in the summer of 1945, in Greece, from where he sent back some interesting letters, he fell ill, and went to hospital with 'heat stroke', and died almost at once—of pulmonary tuberculosis in both lungs. This wasting disease was unsuspected while he lived, for he had seldom gone sick, but went on working through all fatigue and battle strain, literally wearing himself out and losing his life in the service of others.

Devon,   HENRY WILLIAMSON
11 March 1960.

1943
NORTH AFRICA

Tonight I ought to be taking you to the Odeon, or to a pub with latticed windows and locals smoking rich tobacco, but I can get no nearer to you than writing to you. One day I am going to send you a letter packed beginning to end with all the swear words I know, and others far worse which I shall invent. You will know then that I am letting myself go about this bloody war, having lost the control which I am exacting now. I know it will do no good at all beyond easing my blood pressure but when I ponder on life in 1943, and realize that my life with you is connected by this intermittent link of inadequate mail, and that that mail is subject to the rigours of minefields, submarines and censors, then swearing and cat kicking becomes a very necessary outlet.

We are waiting in a certain harbour, I cannot tell you which so I tell you which it is not. Accordingly I have no qualms in telling you that we are not at the great Medway port of Barming, nor are we at Diss on the Waveney. And if I were suddenly granted shore leave tonight I would not go to Kensington, from which you may conclude I am not moored on the Round Pond. We wear life jackets and feel like dowagers or mezzo-sopranos at La Scala, and in the mornings when we are not allowed below we push our upholstered way through crowds of synthetic bosoms. It's quite exhausting and presents a sight like Woolworths on a Saturday night, so that one cannot walk but has rather to steer oneself and make the greater part of the way by wriggles and squirms and sideways shuffles. Were we tubes of toothpaste we would have been squeezed out long ago.

Chopper has just observed that he takes all this with a

pinch of salt. It's such an *Altmark*-ish nightmare existence that he refuses to believe it. We are so closely packed that in our eyes a 'phone booth has become a model home.

Living between decks is as noisy, as crowded, and as uncomfortable as living on a fairground. The fairground analogy is heightened by the fact that very occasionally a loudspeaker tinnily emits a Sousa, *Land of Hope and Glory* and *It's a Long Way to Tipperary*, usually in that order. But worse than anything else is the horrible humid atmosphere. It makes us lethargic and given to sleep. Kit is stuffed into racks, and if one piece is moved usually a lot more clatters down about your ears. I've seen two blokes crowned by tin hats and just before dinner Dapper Price roared at Andy Kirk: 'So it's you who's reading *Pickwick Papers*.' 'Yes,' said Andy, preparing to defend Dickens. 'Any objections?' 'Yes,' he said. 'The damn thing fell on my head three times this morning!'

We are six days out now and no incidents beyond a cockroach in Stan's rabbit stew. Take a pin, my poppet, and closing your lovely eyes, jab it in the map, and if on opening said lovely eyes you find that you have made a mark somewhere in the centre of a censored ocean you're about right. Your husband is doing his washing there, or rather has just done it. At the moment it is fluttering from the rails in company with the colours and smalls of a few hundred others, giving the ship an unjustifiable gala appearance. Among all that lot somebody's mother doesn't use Persil, for I'm afraid my whites are mottled and blotched and look rather like our complexions first day out. Now like most of the others I should be upstairs keeping an eye on it, for 'thieving hooks', as my grandmother has it, abound on the ocean; but Johnny Sutherland is doing that for me.

Food the first day out was rather more plentiful than it has become since, for lots of blokes winced at the sight of it, preferring to hang from the rails upstairs, emptying their stomachs into the sea. My own stomach has done nothing more than go up and down like a ping-pong ball at a shooting gallery. It has hit the back of my teeth so many times that they are all loose and flap in the wind as happily as my washing. Blokes were sick all over the place, 'No wonder they call it the Silent Service,' said stretcher bearer Buffin, 'You daren't open your mouth.' Lenny Jones, who had had four visitations, moaned something to the effect that he wished to be given land, any land, St. Helena or Devil's Island, any place so long as it was land, something with a surface that didn't stand on its end every few seconds. And so it goes on.

29.3.'43

Most of the previous day the distant range of the Sierra Nevadas had stood to port and we had seen its blueness with sprinklings of white villages at the foot, and white veins feeling down the rugged sides; but now, the day before my father's birthday, we waited our turn to put into the harbour and whiled away the time peering through glasses at the white city piling on the hills.

We have landed now. I have seen so much to draw and so much to write that I dither like a weathercock in a whirlwind, not knowing which to tell first, for picking a subject among so many is as difficult as picking the Derby winner. Perhaps as good a method as any is to adopt the time-honoured device of the punter who makes his selection by stabbing a list with a pin. First, says my pin, the foliage. It is such an incredible green, the colours so full blooded, so straight out of the tube with no diluting whatsoever. The sun was sizzling on them all and they screamed back at him, violent, alive—bombing the eyes after the greyness of Scotland. The hill high above the terraces of white buildings was fringed against the skyline by palms and cypresses. Dapper little Javanese stewards from our ship scuttled down the gangway, gave our formed-up battalion hand-waves and gold-toothed smiles and, every flat-footed man jack of them made their sunny way into the city from the dock. Each one was a sartorial dazzler in razor-edged Hollywood styles. Ships were busy coaling and un-loading, sergeant-majors yelled and sent the tide back a hundred yards. We marched out and it ventured in again.

Now it is useless my attempting to give you a pace-by-pace description of the district, for even after a hundred letters I should be kilometres behind and hopelessly out of step. Things would not be related in the order of their importance and that's what should be aimed at. Therefore we will take the Arab. He is not much to take, and if you saw him you would never chide me for having one sock inside out. You'd con-sider your husband a dude and be thankful he has socks, for the average Arab has none at all and less of most things. It has made everyone think. Why is the Arab dressed so often in very carefully patched sacks? Why is he always in so tat-tered a state that in England he'd be turned away from the worst doss houses? Why in this city of lovely buildings is he shut off in native quarters? Is this how the white man brings benefits to the natives? Imperialism has no defence here.

All the time I am seeing so many new things I am wishing

20

you were here, and grow increasingly impatient for the day when our travels begin. You'd revel in all this in spite of the unbelievably evil smells. Brangwyn has painted it all with pre-Raphaelite exactitude and was true after all, and not as I had suspected, overdoing it. I never saw such a collection of carts, ramshackle, rococo, ancient, modern—I expect a Boadicea chariot to turn up any minute complete with knives on the hubs. All this assortment hoots and jingles along and bears such variegated cargoes as oranges, scrap-iron, and yashmak'd wives. The reins or wheels have a motley of handlers from flaccid Frenchmen to lean Arabs that the very horses must be as amazed as I am. Certainly the ensemble makes Bertram Mills's outfit look like a mummers' outing to Grant's tomb on a wet Wednesday. Mingled with all this and bent on I know not what mysterious business are scores of comic-opera troops with fezzes, blue coats, gleaming swords, turbans, belted overcoats and I doubt not the good old Page-Croft Home Guard pike. There are droves of dolorous donkeys with very often an Arab on board, feet nearly touching the floor; there are sheep and goats and scenes stolen from the Bible and still back in that age. And in the middle of these scenes the twentieth century has somehow planted a pylon.

There are many reminders of England. The lark is shrilling his head off. The swallow is here. I've seen several herons and in the ditches are our wild flowers in as brave an array as anywhere in Kent. The gallant red campion is here, the mallow stands above hosts of daisies. I like them better than the exotics, and I picked one to send to you, but won't; for if it's not censored, it'll be put into quarantine.

We couldn't eat at the swanky American joint, nor get
beyond the front door, and the Church Army dump situated
in what I took to be a former night-club—'another victory
won for God,' said Maxie—served such tasteless tea in
such dirty mugs that God Himself could be little elated with
victory, and like us hoped it would soon be a night-club
again. We set out to find something with less of the silver
lady and charity atmosphere about it. We saw George Parker
and three other sergeants in a café and they were beaming so
much and seemed to be having such a regal time, that we
applied a shoulder to the press just inside the door and forced
an entry. From which you will gather it was well patronized,
very well patronized, your chair pressed against the back of
someone else's chair. It was packed like a school treat, so
George Parker and Co. stepped through the window because
it was easier than going through the door. Also they saved
about half an hour of time that way. Don't worry, they
didn't break the window, our boys aren't rowdy as a rule,
there just wasn't any window there. Where plate glass used
to be was just the hole. I got right alongside that hole, for
though I felt I was practically sitting on the pavement, I
figured it was a good O.P. for drawing. And while Maxie
aired his French and made no impression and Andrew did the
same and nearly got himself involved in a duel, I managed to
do one drawing already on the way to you—what time the
boys had already got the first part of the meal ordered. Noses
down, they were sipping, rather noisily—though it didn't
matter in the general din—the foulest soup I've ever tasted. It

had round things in it like white washers, I think it was nothing more than stagnant washing-up water. Even the French name it had didn't get it by. Then the chubby French waitress wriggled her way through the chairs to present us with a dish of entrails, though she called them 'choux fleur'. Also there was *oeuf* and *pomme-de-terre* omelette and more spuds in a dish, some bread and *vin blanc* which made Jack Steeel's smile wider than ever and Lenny rub his hands till the sparks flew. I didn't enjoy it in the least and at that moment I thought with less disfavour of your cheese concoctions. All the same I would not have missed that meal, for the fact that it was in semi-public made it interesting. Not only to us but to almost everybody in North Africa. Sailors, searching about for a place, would pull up and ask us what it was like. Soldiers would do the same. And what did it cost they said. Our open window was like an inquiry office. For some time a quiet little Arab boy had been gazing wistfully at the table with his head resting against the woodwork of the window. And very soon, two more, saucier, came along with newspapers. They also stood watching and they too asked for food. We gave them some and the waitress flew up to the table excitably shooing them away like Betsy Trotwood dismissing the donkeys from her lawn at Dover. But they came back again. So did another one, a bootblack this time who, extending a brush which was obviously fighting a losing battle with dandruff, intimated that he wished to clean our boots. All the time colourful people were passing, shrouded women, black-dressed Frenchwomen with baskets, comic-opera troops, a continual parade of all the stage costume since the days of the Roman theatre. And inside there was the clatter and chatter of the diners, the smell of the food and thick curls of tobacco smoke. Two

23

French officers stepped through our window, pitched their hats on to a rack and squeezed into a table in the corner. Then a top note split the atmosphere and there was a dark tenor with side-boards and the fingers of his left hand drumming his bosom while he unburdened in the manner operatic with everything save tone.

With him was a little man with a colossal accordion, a fat man, who pulled the accordion right round him, shut it up again and then extended it so wide that the diners had to lean over to one side. You never heard such a racket in all your life. I was roaring with laughter, so were the others, while Jack's smile threatened to decapitate him. Suddenly a shadow loomed in at the window and a Frenchman let out a chain of folding photographs of this town across the table as though he were throwing streamers. 'Allez,' we said in masterly French, but it wasn't until we gave the American translation and a coarser Cockney one and said 'scram' and 'B—— off' that we got rid of him. He was replaced almost at once by another chap with a basket of 'Souvenirs, M'sieur?' He was followed by a tray of something in conical packets—almonds, sherbet or something. Then like a zombi, he seemed to rise from the ground, there appeared a most hideous blind beggar, an Arab. He had a black crestfallen moustache, wet at the ends, and awful sunken sockets for eyes; within one a tiny gleam of pupil showed dull and evil, like water in a disfigured well. He passed his tin in and with head sideways listened for dropping francs. He went, leaving us somewhat sobered. You can't eat when you see such things.

Now into the ring of Arab boys who had been at the window all the time there sauntered a French boy, the cockiest, most self-possessed and funniest I've ever seen. He pushed back the head of the nice quiet Arab boy with his hand, and I was prepared to be brusque with him but his ludicrous manner quite disarmed me. He minced up and down the pavement, to the kerb and back again, in and out the circle of Arabs. He was fair and looked like a juvenile Stan Laurel though without the timidity. He did conjuring tricks with a thimble, swallowing it and making it appear out of his waistcoat. He did this for some time, ignoring the water the waitress flung at the group with fine scorn, lifting his nose as the artist might at the boys who yell 'Get your hair cut'.

There came yet another beggar. He gave us a broad gaptoothed Arab smile, came stiffly to attention in rags and bare feet. He saluted, held the position, quivering for a full minute; then beamed, pointing first to himself and then to us, saying: 'Allies.' After which he pointed to the food: 'Take no notice of him,' someone said, 'or he'll keep on doing it.' So I didn't, but he kept on. At last I gave him some bread, and he pointed to the lettuce. The boys extended their hands too. It was too much for us. We gave away what was left. There was a pitiful scramble for it, and we had to restrain our saluting ally to make sure the kids got an equal share.

The meal in that dim, noisy and crowded café cost 28 francs apiece—about three shillings.

8.4.'43

When it rains here it comes down in buckets, tin baths and static-water tanks. Two non-stop days we had of it, and we sploshed in mud so liquid that it was tidal. Chopper told me he picked up a tin hat and one of the guard was under it, but Chopper always exaggerates. And among all that we were told to bath. Undressing to avoid getting muddy was an involved business. I think I put one foot in the water, cold, and pulled my trousers over my head. A performance I doubt if I could repeat. Then the business of drying, a race between the towel and the rain. You didn't get dry, but if you rubbed vigorously you did get less wet. Though I doubt if we were less dirty for it.

Sometimes I went ankle deep in mud, my feet looking something like martins' nests, only much, much larger. I had given up seeing my boots, but when I went into a nearby suburb I found the mud didn't deter the dozens of Arab boot-boys. To them I represented trade, and they buzzed after me as if I were a queen bee. 'Two francs, Johnny,' (we are all Johnnies here) and so on the steps of the Y.M.C.A., where young Abdul got busy with scraper, brush and ersatz velvet. Several others continued to solicit my custom despite Abdul's being on the first boot.

If Private Snelling doesn't pin his ears to the ground as I advise him to, of course he'll slide down the hill, and of course he'll have to get up in the middle of the night and walk back to where his blankets are; this sleeping on a mountain side is a tricky business. I sleep with Stan in a crosswise trench which checks our rolling, but it is seldom a comfortable night for he has so many bones, corners and edges that I feel that I am sleeping in a knife box.

We've had a couple of quiet days here, though a couple of Junkers 109 came grazing fiercely round the mountain side; in that way they come upon us suddenly. So close were they that Stan and Bill didn't see them, in fact they didn't expect them to come skimming across the top of the sage. But I got in a shot at one. My first at a Fascist; and to my undying shame

26

I must confess that I did not bring him down. You will nag me, I know, and I shan't protest because I feel I deserve it.

We have been living in foxholes for days now and our only chance of getting boots and clothes off is during quiet periods of the day. I've just had a bath in a sooty tin on this Djebel, and the wind sweeping across made the towel redundant. But I think we'll want a dozen turkish baths when we leave here!

Night is closing in, and I must prepare my foxhole for sleep, or rather a blanket-pulling tussle with Stan.

16.4.'43

I have just managed to get an airgraph back for posting to you after four days of endeavour. We are front-line troops now and it complicates things a little. The day is westering and I have a green envelope to fill for you. I shall probably fill it with odds and ends. Had my pen been more fluid there would have very likely been a splash here for I had to dive into a slit trench while a couple of Stukas roared down the valley. Couldn't get a shot in, they keep clear of Gunn's gun. Remember that Sunday in Bexley Road when the machine-gun clips came tumbling down through the trees around us? Very much like that here and yesterday I was sprawled face-down—limpeting a hill—terrible—while a plane dived. Bullets kicked up the earth and I thought they'd pass across my outstretched legs. But they're rotten shots. Life, if a bit raw, you can wash only sometimes, is not uneventful, and I think you would like it and certainly Goo, who has an iron nerve, would.

I put a lovely flower in here for you, a tranquil little thing, something like our crowding stitchwort, which surprisingly

enough I have never seen in Kent though in Essex they throng
the woods and ditches as though it were permanently market
day in those places. I found a few of these flowers along a
bank side near Newmarket, but a local told me they were not
wild flowers but garden flowers that strayed through the front
gate. But he called them by the loveliest name—Star of
Bethlehem. It is sprinkled here and there upon this Djebel
(mountain) and glows as gentle and calm as the evening star.
I have put one in the envelope but alas, when you pull a star
down from the sky its lustre wanes, and it is the same with
my flower.

It looks like Montgomery will be in Tunis before we are,
though we in the First Army are nearer. But please don't
blame us. We are fighting through mountains and Jerry
holds on grimly. He is gradually going back though, hill by
hill, thanks mainly to our obvious superiority in artillery
which sends over some deadly barrages. It's blowing up
mighty cold just now. The sun has dipped behind the ridge
just across the way. Contrary weather here, during the day
you can't move for heat, at night you can't keep still for
shivering. My blanket, which I carry across my shoulders
when marching, in the manner of the 8th Route Army is
bloody well threadbare.

Another insertion for the envelope—a nice piece torn from
a German newspaper I found here. It is good to march
through these gullies and gulches and find broken and dis-
carded enemy equipment. Andrew put on a German helmet,
and my word, I begin to suspect him. He really does look the
part. We came upon a plane mangled almost beyond recognition, and we had already seen three come down that day.
We passed a grave here and there, one in a ditch beside a

concertina-ed truck and carrier. A rough, wooden, anonymous cross stuck from it. A cow with ribs rotting through was nearby. On the slope where Percy Ross is at the moment there is another grave, somebody of the 5th Buffs says the pencil marks on the wood 'killed in action.' The other evening I went up to write something on it, something I thought perhaps his folks would like, but the shelling which started then compelled me to retreat. I had occasion to thank the underground movement then for the whistle came again as I was going across open ground. I was prone in an instant and a shell thudded alongside me, and didn't explode! We had quite a bit of shelling that day. They tried for our observation post first, high on a ridge. There were four of us in it, a stone structure not sensibly chosen at all. We curled up half a dozen times while shots whistled over and sat up waiting for the next one. Then a big fat ball of plush buzzed through—a bee looking like one of the 2s. 6d. seats at the Odeon without the ashtray—one of the officers flattened himself again. He smiled a bit sheepishly afterwards, but it shows how finely the senses get attuned. Altogether I think we were subjected to five bouts of shelling that day but amazingly there was only one casualty apart from two cases of cut hands. Percy Ross, Frank Robinson and Arthur Stevens lifted him out of his hole with the greatest of difficulty, for ironically it was the narrowest, the deepest and the safest trench of the lot. Shrapnel had gone right through his helmet. He had a compound fracture of the skull but has a chance of pulling through, I am told. Percy, Frank and Steve did good work there, for all the time they were bearing the chap away, shells were still coming over. They couldn't flatten every time but stood still, freezing so to speak with hunched shoulders and bated breath.

You would have chided me for my 'trench'. You see I was supposed to be in the O.P. on the height but that was their main target and I had been driven from it. Still, I had to establish another when I could, so instead of squatting in a trench I sat in what was merely a large earthen saucer with a lance-corporal for company, a can of petrol, a Jerry machine-gun in working order and with yards of bullet belts. Outside the hole the ground was plotted with more sinister holes where the stuff was landing. But the spirit of the boys was fine. Out in no-man's-land of the open, tea was brewing up and they were more concerned with the safety of that can of water than anything else. 'We'll fix bayonets and go after the bastard if he upsets that,' they said.

Another time I was in the stretcher bearer's hole eating stewed apricots, navvy fashion, with Frank Robinson and Steve—that is to say, having a spoonful each in turn out of the same dixie like navvies swinging hammers—when he started it over again. That meant that if you kept upright while the others ducked they missed a go and you had two dips, but none of us thought it worth while taking the chance.

I wrote to our Bonnie Mary the other day that I was surprised, pleasantly so, by the casual air that pervades the front, but that was before we got any bad shelling. Even so there is no reason to amend the pronouncement (I talk like a town crier, don't I?) for between things there's a lovely bank holiday atmosphere about everything. If there's a stream—which there isn't at the moment—blokes will have a stand-up bath in it, trusting in the sportiness of the Stukas not to choose such a sitting target should they come over. I had a lovely bath the other day. Your spouse standing in a mountain stream dressed in nothing but his identity disc made a pic-

ture that would be a prime attraction for the screen. Chaps
are sunbathing here and there or drumming up, and Potter,
our pocket Hercules, comes bouncing across the ruts and
ridges in his jeep, treating the thing like a Spitfire. He's having
an immense time out here though he was shaken the other
day when he was Stuked along a road and saw a chap in
front of him killed by a mortar bomb.

'You two look like Burke and Hare,' commented Andrew
as Stan and I were digging an O.P. in the moonlight. 'Yes,' I
said, 'And no doubt my spouse is telling herself what a lovely
romantic night it is while we are cussing it.' For O.P.s must
be dug in positions within the enemy's arc of vision, relying
purely on camouflage to go undetected. Shells, ours, were
whistling over our heads and Jerry planes were hanging up
parachute flares, lighting up the country over a wide radius
so that several times we had to go flat and wait till the flares
had completed their almost imperceptible descent.

It was a ten-mile climb to this place, and having completed
it, Andrew commented on the fantastic nature of our situation. 'Did you, in your wildest dreams, ever imagine a scene
like this,' I summed up. 'Here we are, you, Bill, Stan and I,
squatting under the moon and calm stars, with the air heavy
with the scent of sage, on the highest mountain in Tunisia,
miles away from home and all eating bully beef off a plate
marked N.A.A.F.I. It is kind of unreal, eh?'

I saw a sight the other day which made me write to Mary
forthwith, for she would have loved to have witnessed it.
Maxie and Oscar Wynn came along the ridge from 'A' Company with Anton Muller and Leopold Drexter—our very
first prisoners. They had given themselves up, creeping out of
the hills fluttering a white handkerchief. Both were N.C.O.s,

31

and Andrew, who had to question them, found that the one who wore the Russian ribbon had been to Kharkov and had been wounded at the approaches to Stalingrad. Both looked fed up and neither the brutal Nazi; one, a fair youth with a soft mouth, had flowers pressed in his notebook. But it was good that Maxie should bring in the first prisoners.

20.4.'43

Wisps of mist have gone, the conjuror of the morning has whipped away the white veils and the hills are exposed. Tawny light gilds the left eye of George Parker, his jack-knife bobs on his khaki buttocks as he passes beneath the shadows. The convoy grunts and revs to the road, on the move! Beja ahead, a white town switching over the hills. Up on the left hay is collected in small mounds over the field like rivets, for all the world as if you could remove the rivets, roll up the whole green field and bear it away to the jewel salvage centre. Fields and more fields, corn and barley and a child cutting it with a sickle, often working side by side with a combine. Two Arabs ride on a white horse with a tail like a waterfall, they wear a contrast in hats, one a red skull cap, the other a wide, shadow-making Mexican hat of yellow straw. Overdomed Yanks, goggled like beetles, buzz by in jeeps, one, two, three, four. Some sit over the back as though on a field latrine. The truck bellies canvas as it overtakes a trailing six-pounder with a squaddie holding his hat on. Don R's pass, looking like beetles or ant-men, the chin pieces of their crash helmets flap outwards like leather Dundrearys. There are slumped signs at Hindenburg Corner.

There's a poppy, shining! The sun in its wide bonnet.

Small plants like bulrushes, blue busbies charging the ditch.
A dip, a new horizon, always new horizons, chasing horizons,
like happiness always out of reach. Passing lorries lean away
from each other and a wedge of sky balances on its point
between. There's an Arab driving a white horse in a trap, his
head high, arched neck and mane a tugging banner, Jerry
prisoners pass in a troop transport, wearing Afrika Corps
hats, some with peaks turned up Ak-Ak wise, every head
turned to look in on us. Their national colour buttons are like
a bell-push, press and a Nazi idea answers. What do they think
of us—Steve lying on camouflage netting struggling with the
jolting print of *Lorna Doone*, hair on his legs like gold filings
in the sun, me writing?

The trucks pull off the road and trickle through a gap in
the cactus hedge into an olive grove; reminds me of cows
going in to be milked. Ah, those were real things, I can still
smell that lovely smell, sour milk, I can almost feel their warm
sides and blunt, snotty noses. It magic-carpets me right back
to England, to Chelmsford and the sketching of them in the
noisy market place. And there was fat Rosemary of the Agri-
cultural College, fat with bouncing good humour, standing
at a five-bar gate between Galley Wood and shady Stock, and
calling 'Come on, me darlings', and they coming to her
from right across the field. Good 'ole Rosie' she certainly
had a way with cows. They would beg for her, give milk
for her, even lay eggs for her and the one that jumped over
the moon certainly did it for Rosemary.

We've done over a hundred miles now and I haven't mentioned camels. They're not seen here, but were common at
the start of the journey. Working wells, ploughing side by
side with oxen or pulling two-wheeled carts. With their

C   33

curved profile and droop lids they're the Melborn Inman of animals, tattered and proud. Aristocrats in rags, a monocle wouldn't be out of place, slow and dignified yes, but comic dignity, Chaplin dignity. Their feet are comical too, they splodge along like pancakes, rubber hoofs like feet in sacks. I think of a Jewess whose ankles ooze over her shoes splodging in the bathroom. Poor camel, poor Jewess, come to that.

25–30.4.'43

I thought that two of my toes had escaped but they were merely lizards darting from underfoot. There are hundreds of them, and the fields are a festival of flowers, but for all that your mention of chestnuts abloom in a letter I received yesterday made all this pale, and I had a fierce nostalgia for home and was reminded particularly of Findon in Sussex which had the finest chestnuts I know. It is Easter bank holiday today and all are frizzling on the Djebel and in the plain. Transport going along the road trails a high dust screen, it hangs and you'd think it was a fire. But tonight there is no time for details for being holiday time to morrow we go for an outing. I cannot say anything about it beyond that it will be lively.

The fine sieve of the censorship would let little through if I told you what I want to. And what I have seen makes it difficult for me to write. I would appeal to the censor for permission to tell you that there are good boys, heroes, whom we shall never see again—so that you might be spurred to greater efforts in the factory, in the fight against apathy, in all the necessary fights back home to achieve the things necessary for the assurance of victory and the ending of this ghastly

34

war. Beyond that I will say nothing except that I and all the fellows you met are safe, though Pomfret and Pilgrim prisoners and Maxie back somewhere with a foot wound. The photo I sent you of the stretcher bearers I request you give place of honour to on the screen. They are tops, though Chopper told me that it was only thoughts of Stalingrad that kept him going. But that need not be taken literally for Chopper always has been and always will be a hundred per cent without that. And they are all like Chopper.

4.6.'43

Ten letters all at once—disappointingly, a mere three from you. But they were lovely. And you're proud. Gosh. I'd like to see you now. I think we'd both talk a thousand to the minute and both at the same time so that neither of us heard half. Shall I tell you something to make you even more proud? I haven't told anyone else. And first I should warn you that nothing might come of it—only I've been recommended for a decoration! I don't know what, only it's nothing very big. They sent my name up some time ago. I don't want it except for the reason that you might be more pleased and that it proves that I don't funk anything—and that is what everybody is afraid of before they go in. Nothing spectacular but for general example. I guess I could not have shown that example had I not disobeyed orders for I was ordered to stay back. That part pleases me but won't please you so much for I remember your arguments, but I claim that certain circumstances justify it.

You ask me not to mess up your future. I thought a lot of your future, our wonderful plans out there. Steve, Chopper, and I were going up to the Tunis Road for casualties. An occasional bullet would snarl across, and it grew warmer as we went on. We found a casualty, creeping along the ditch. 'Let Chopper go back with him, Steve,' I said. I was glad to get Chopper back out of it. Steve and I went on—on our bellies by now. We came to a knocked-out Churchill tank and a Black Watch carrier. Merry was behind the tank, Lt. Glynn and Balderston in a jeep with his head bandaged. A bullet plucked Glynn's shirt and he got farther behind. Merry was using some of his best night-club language. He was good. Steve and I crawled on in a ditch that was all too shallow. Steve, back with the next casualty, a difficult job because every time you disturbed the grass they'd send something whining across to where they judged you were. They had eyes like lynx, those guys.

Now Fishenden was hit farther up. Where 'farther up' was, I didn't know. You didn't know where anything was in front —or what. The ditch flattened out and I crawled left into the corn, which, though hiding me from view, didn't stop bullets. And I'm clumsy and awkward, I flurried the corn. 'Ping-ping', whizzing mosquitoes from Krupps and Skoda. I heard them cutting through the corn. That's when I thought of your future. I rested my forehead on the ground, for it was painful, crawling, and below the larger noises of projectiles I could hear the ticking of insects, the notes of the lark fell around me in a silver shower and the sun was hot on my neck. My fingers clawed the ground. Shall I go on? I asked that question out loud. I don't know where anyone is, I am isolated. Jerry is where?—On the right and in front—but how near? But Fish is out there too. I thought of our future, our happy times. Back, going back was your future and immediate failure—going back was failure. You gave me your answer. 'Fish! Fish!' I yelled, and I ran up the road in spurts for crawling was hellish. Run and down, crawl a bit in case I'm covered —up—run and down, ah, the ditch has appeared again. Fish! Bet I'm running right into Jerry—ping—ya missed! Fish! Why, here's the pioneers. 'My, Nick, am I glad to see you —where's Fish? H'ya, Jack, h'ya, Jimmy, h'ya, Nick, you're pinned, I suppose. Bloody warm—eh?' 'Yes, we won't be able to get out of here till dusk, Fish is over the road.' I doubled across. Then we made imprints of ourselves in the ground for they machine-gunned then. 'Bastards.' Nick started padding across the road on all fours. 'Great life this,' he laughed. 'So long—I'll be seeing you—perhaps.' I told him for Christ's sake get up and run. He did and got safely over. A sergeant, Nick, a good boy—we'll have him round one evening when we get back.

Fish was lying on his back, not badly hurt, but shaken and in need of a rest more than anything. Crawling back was difficult and we went 20 yards and stopped exhausted. 'How about trying to walk, Fish?' I said. 'They're rotten shots.' 'I'm game.' So slowly, with his arm about my shoulders we struggled on. 'Jerry might not shoot if he sees you're a casualty.' Jerry answered that with bullets and we were down again. It went on like that for some time but we got in eventually.

Rumour awarded you a pension. Rumour revving up at H. Q. had killed me at 'B' Echelon. This came about, I suppose, because at dawn I would leave H.Q.—for the Intelligence Section simply wasn't functioning—and go up front with the stretcher bearers—to which now I officially belong. It was often evening before I reappeared. Andrew would

37

annoy me. 'You've got to eat,' he'd say, 'and sleep, Sergeant, make him eat something.' But I couldn't eat much and sleep only meant living the day all over again. But I'm shooting a line. A disgusting letter altogether. I'll pack up and do some drawing for you.

21–26.6.'43

It is, as usual, a hot enervating day, and to write a letter is a task. For four days I've put it off. I'm sorry and I don't know the real reason for it, for there has been plenty of physical effort, swimming and three games of football in two days! And another one this evening. But I get day-long bouts of thorough aversion towards anything that involves the slightest mental effort, though I like the swimming and football. I know that above all it is a way of escape. This letter is awful, I feel it. I feel as though the sun has got in my head, and all the roads my thoughts run along are sticky with tar bubbles. Thoughts and reflections flash and dazzle, my mind is puffy and florid, seeking an ice-cream parlour and finding it not. It is all unrealist. It is all damnable.

You must pardon my letters now that they are miserable things, written when I ought not to attempt writing, but I think the depression is dispersing now. The cause of the depression? I don't know really—a host of contributing causes probably and perhaps part of the slow reaction to those hectic days of battle. But I suppose I'm an emotional sort of person, though not demonstrative, I mean that I don't dance and flop about in a crisis, in fact I was, I'm relieved to say, a remarkably cool person in those days. I'm given to feeling more than thinking and can't always say what I feel. And I was a strange, bleak sort of guy then whom I wonder at now, who ate little and slept less, who departed each dawn with just a rifle and bandolier. If this sounds a little heroic, as I'm afraid it does, I'd better say that I performed no heroisms, or if what I did can be called that it was because I had joined a group whose behaviour was an example to the whole battalion. My leaving my old unit was no indictment of inefficiency, that group, after the first day, simply didn't function, in fact the only time something was required of it, it had returned to H.Q. and I had to fill the bill. But the stretcher bearers were hard pressed and I felt that I had to go and help them out.

We were around Sidi Abdullah, a few miles east of Medjez-el-Bab and here as you must surely have read was the most bitter fighting of the whole campaign—including El Alamein, and among all that I was a strange sort of person, feeling dumbly, and perhaps now I am unwinding with the effects of events hinted at in those last two letters. I'm sorry I had to inflict this on you but maybe the process has finished now. Let's forget it.

The writing is on the wall. Not in the prognostic sense, but in white chalk on the wall of the Nissen hut that serves as cookhouse. A Yank put in yesterday. He came from Rochester, N.Y., studied for opera, had Italian parents and knew their language. The writing was the conjugation of certain verbs in Italian. Italians cook for us here and sometimes it's a dickens of a job to make them understand. Our staff is small, just enough to run a transit camp and we are quite distinct from the rest of the battalion who are about three hundred yards away. Pino is favourite among the Italians. He's all smiles and so eager to please. They wait on us at meals, cook splendidly, wash up for us and give the impression that they'd be offended if we did it ourselves. They're happy working here but I don't like the being-waited-upon business. Seems to me like taking unfair advantage of our position and it inflates us with a feeling of being *Herrenvolk*. Or it might. But the atmosphere is one of fun and friendliness. Pino is short, has round brown, rolling eyes, gestures much with his hands and shoulders and a sideways incline of his round head. His hair is short and black, his smile is wide and white and very ready. My caricatures of Roosevelt and Musso amused him greatly and when I started a sly one of him, he saw, laughed loudly and plumped down on to the bench in a pose. 'Caricatura profilo,' he chuckled, and putting his hand to his nose pulled it out as though it was invisible spearmint. In this way he indicated the anticipated exaggeration. The picture is on the wall now. He is a likeable little chap, Pino, and about as warlike as a dove. In case you should imagine a scene of Irish linen and sparkling silver when I told you we were being waited on, let me point out that our tables are packing cases.

This morning I had my hair cut by a prisoner barber. A Fascist razor scraping my neck! But these ordinary blokes are all right and all the boys have said for a long time that we should never be fighting them, that there is a basis for a permanent peace between ordinary peoples. In fact, Vansittart won't wash here for the same goes for Germans too. Sometimes we have to work the prisoners, actually we call for volunteers from them and they come eagerly—I had four of them squatting round my tent and we taught each other certain nouns with the aid of drawings. The four of them carried my kit from the tent (for I was shifting into the ration store where I am supposed to be storeman) safari fashion, and we all sang excerpts from *Aida* and *Tosca*. Verra goodo! Verra La Scala Milano.

To get this away I must finish now. It's not very satisfactory, but I'll follow with another today.

30.6.'43

A truck and a jeep came up and the American band got out, took their seats on ration boxes and began tuning up. The blokes plopped down on the slope—twos and threes came over the skyline and swelled the numbers. The Italian prisoners lined the wire of their cage. Pino, Mario, and Eduardo came out of the cookhouse where they work. The latter two sat alongside me outside the Nissen hut. Pino sat a little in front on the concrete border of the grease trap. His chin rested heavily in his hands. The band started with the brass and the saxophones moaning low. The tuba added its deeper note. The faces of the audience were poker red in the waning day. The Italians by the wire were silent, attentive. I looked at little Pino. It was cruel. His great brown eyes, his whole mien were sad. He was home again in Tripoli. I would not have remarked upon it had a tear rolled down his cheek. I expected it. I have felt starved for music out here but it hurts when you hear it, even jazz. The first number ended, there was a momentary pause; then the stupor went and dreams of home were shattered before a thousand clapping hands.

George Parker came over and squeezed between Eduardo and me. Eduardo put his arm round George's shoulders. That's how it is here. We of the little transit camp and the Italians of the cookhouse have become real friends. They are sad when they talk of going away, or of us going away as one day we must. George is perhaps their great favourite for he is a like-able bloke with an easy first approach. He's a sergeant, but quite a number of our sergeants are not of the stage type. He regrets that he didn't meet you, but he'll be one of our most frequent visitors some day. I indicated Pino. 'We've probably killed quite a lot of Pino's, George!'

'Yes, and they've killed a lot of our Pino's—isn't it all nonsensical and futile.'

'And we'll kill a lot more Pino's, George.'

'And they'll kill a lot more of our Pino's—and the tragedy is that there's no other way out until they get rid of some of the ideas.'

'Who gave them the ideas, George, they would never arise if we mingled with the Pino's more often.' And before the band wailed again we decided that only a mingling with the Pino's will find the answer—the answer will only come from the common people and a studying of their interests.

It was George's birthday today and on his mess-tin this morning he found a card to Sgt. Giorgio Parker. It was a photo of Roman ruins and on the back was written 'Happi Birthday—Buon Compleanno—Pino and Eduardo'.

Following the band there was a film show. Cigarettes shone in the dark. The screen swung in the wind. Cars ran on buckled wheels and husky footballers tore about on rickety legs and kept husky. And the States launched the most un-seaworthy vessel ever, that bending screen was a most expert saboteur. For an outdoor screen the sound was remark-ably clear, especially when I recall Army indoor cinema shows in which the human voice was represented by a sound like a blackberry bush being pulled down a tin chimney.

Bob Scott, who is R.S.M. of the transit camp, Frank Robinson and I drank to the third year of the formation of the
Shambler Platoon. Arthur Stevens, although not of our
original platoon, joined on the same day in the next platoon.
He was there too. We were all sprawled in the medical tent,
lying on stretchers. Bob poured out whisky, which sergeants
can obtain—and I, as chief Shambler, was called upon to make
a speech. A lackadaisical sort of celebration but the air is too
hot and the limbs so heavy here that Percy, George, Chopper,
Harry Routledge, Jack Snell and the few others that remain
wouldn't have come along had we arranged it—the Shamblers
hate any sort of ceremony and the separation of the transit
camp from the rest of the battalion made it difficult. 27th June
—three years ago, we were given trousers that looked like
Japanese lanterns and great armoured boots that went down
Gabriel's Hill at Maidstone several seconds before we did. All
of us, at some time, have been seized with the impulse to
sit thuddingly down and without ceremony on that slope.
Some of us bear the marks to this day. The 'great interruption'
Sitwell calls it. Many of us were on the verge of careers,
halfway through apprenticeships—all of us have to start
again.

I am pleased to say that all the Shamblers were top-notch
in action. The other day I had my first news of the reaction
of one of them. A chap told me of a certain fellow who had
completely been passed over in promotions and is still a
lance-corporal, while his behaviour in action and when he was
taken prisoner was such that he should have been promoted
sergeant forthwith. 'Which lance-corporal was that?' 'Jackie
Rudling.' Only one Shambler was killed—Bertie Povah.
Freddie Smith was wounded. Our lazy commemoration of

43

the anniversary left me so hazy that I had to sleep the night where I was.

2.7.'43

Your letter telling me about your visit to the Zoo with Jock reminds me that I once spent a very enjoyable day at Tyrwhitt-Drake's Zoo with Ruth. I had called for you but you were out gallivanting, so it was Ruth. The pelicans were motionless and we heard many comments of amazement as we sat on the bench. 'Look, George, like stone aren't they!' 'Look at those birds, how still they are!' 'Crikey, Charlie, look at those pelicans, don't bat an eyelid, wouldn't think they was human would yer!' We went along to Allington then and drank a cool beer at the Malta and watched the boats joggling on the glinting Medway. The sky was yellow behind the slim poplars. When you dream of the future, you think of sunshine, of rustling leaves and always such evenings as these. We shall have many.

So we have a blanket now and our bottom drawer is getting a tight squeeze? 'Tis well. The bed problem may be solved by hubby snaffling a couple of stretchers. And as to the furniture, please yourself, girl—anything so long as it's comfortable, although we must have one of your Penenden Heath chairs with books in. That was a grand thing wasn't it? When I design some furniture and we get it made we'll have a Guy Fawkes night of the old stuff or mebbe if you don't like the designs it will be a Guy Fawkes night of the new stuff. But my favourite piece of furniture is that screen and I've a feeling that you've scrapped that.

How would you like me to take up boxing as a career? Nor

would I. The Pioneers challenged the S.B.s last week. It got round and the boxing pundits of the battalion took a hand and rigged up a pukka ring and elected judges of repute. It flabbergasted us. We wanted a crooked ref., a second who was prepared to put chloroform into the sponge of our opponent, and to have it out quietly away from the crowd so that we could use our own rules and foul to our black hearts' delight. Instead, here was this seething concourse and Madison Square Garden atmosphere. Still, it went off splendidly. Percy won, Chopper won, the Pioneers won two and mine was the last and deciding bout. I fought Cpl. Barton, known as 'Scruff'. It was a grand battle, very enjoyable—every now and then we'd break into a waltz. It was hilarious and the crowd loved it. But I lost—lost points for clowning, they said. Good Lord! Max Baer would never have won a fight in the Army! I put in for extra rations next day, two steaks, one for each eye.

We left the transit camp the other day and did a hundred-mile journey in open trucks. We drove through glorious country with overhanging rocks and deep gorges, but the sun was so hot that we all had thundering heads by the time the journey was ended. Little Pino was there to see us off, waving and saluting and shouting something which we couldn't understand. On our last night we had a drink in the Nissen and Pino was happy and talkative for periods and sad and quiet for others. We were all sorry to leave him and I hope that Ben in Italy is being treated as we treated Pino.

This new camp is near the sea and swimming is the main recreation—you have to if you wish to keep cool. The sands are so hot that you can't stand on them with bare feet. We have pup tents, but they're no protection. In them you ripen like a tomato in a greenhouse. These days the problem is not what to write but where to write. There should be a writing tent with tables and later there might be, but at the moment every letter means a backache, for you perch on forms and packing cases and write on your knees. But I don't write that as an excuse. I'm getting back some more fluency now—after the first impact of the fighting is past.

Now I hear the dinner bell, must go now, for do I not love my dinner more than my wife? Sure I do.

PS. Sure I *don't*—it's corned beef.

4.7.'43

Personally, I do not care for coppers, but I believe in being courteous to them at all times, so when Johnny Brannigan comes into Mindy's restaurant one Friday evening and sits down in the same booth as me because there are no other vacant seats in the joint, I give him a huge hello. Furthermore, I offer him a cigarette and say how pleased I am to see how well he is looking, although as a matter of fact Johnny Brannigan looks very terrible, what with big black circles under his eyes and his face thinner than somewhat——.

No, I guess that method won't do. You know, it's Runyon a mile off, but the fact is I want to write to you, but I can't scrape up much to say unless I muster things from other letters I have written which will look like cheating. But as this is your paper coming right back at you from the pad you sent me and it is American Independence Day, I think I must write to you even if it does resolve into a bald-faced lifting from books. But I am missing you so that I feel I ought to look like Johnny Brannigan anyway with circles round my eyes like Ming the Panda. Instead of which I suppose I am disgustingly healthy, what with the swimming every day and the sun tanning me Sioux colour. And maybe I've hit upon it with my mention of those Injuns. Mebbe the sun gives us, besides a Sioux colour, other Sioux characteristics too, and that accounts for the tendency for letter writing to become difficult. Soon I shall be writing: Dear Spouse,

Ugh. Ugh.

Your ROBBIE.

PS. Ugh. Think there might be something in it?

You sent me some lovely books and I fight a desire to read them or write this. Not that this is a task I kick against, I mean mainly against my inability to say things.

Eggleton watched a ship go right along the skyline today. It dwindled to a dot and vanished. He slumped on to the sand, feeling, he said, like Robinson Crusoe. They'll be lighting bonfires on the beach yet and tying their shirts to poles. Oh, for the ship marked home! Somebody has just said it is Saturday, and everyone else has said: 'Is it?' We seldom know. The drifting days have nothing to distinguish the one from the next, except when the Padre supplies the weekly orientation of a church parade. Saturday used to be such a day too, the highlight of the week. It meant coconut squares over at Rawlins at one time, and ice creams when Colletta came round with his somnambulating horse and gay awning. Later the rush to the Spurs and the crush to get out, with your feet seldom reaching the ground in the surge. And at Maidstone it meant the release from the factory, that was the main significance of Saturday. All over the country the great industrial dams burst and poured out frothing workers to seek the

channels of their own choosing. But to all it was the weekly
bank holiday, the little Xmas. And between Saturday and
Monday there was always the comfortable buffer of the
Sunday to insulate us from the creeping ogre of the following
week. The Saturday as we know it is one of our great losses.
It is one of the treasures we are fighting to get back. I think
one might inspire a flagging Army with that thought—the
recognition that Fascism has stolen our Saturdays.

For the time being this is all if I am to catch the post, but I
know you want letters and will try to make them more
frequent.

9.7.'43

The narrow strip from the sea to the hills is as flat as the
fens and your beloved Holland, and veils of shimmering heat
give it the appearance of some submarine world, a world
set in the sea bed and covered with the pellucid waters of the
southern seas. This shimmering of the air is so pronounced
and so general that it seems to me that I might start from the
truck in which I am sitting and move horizontally, swimming
through it with luxurious lazy strokes. And through the vine-
yard where the grapes are prolific in tight green clusters, I see,
now and then, natives pass under the sleeping trees and they
wear bright hats of yellow straw, blue trousers, and should by
rights have sabots on their feet stuffed with straw, and perhaps
an ear missing, for each one dressed vividly as he is and passing
impersonally through such a vibrant scene, brings to mind
the Van Gogh we see in his picture of the artist going to
paint. To the left of this scene is a group of willows by Corot,
misty and blue, and the telegraph pole of the road past which

48

a donkey is passing, and another cone of straw hat buckles through the distorted mirror of the unceasing shimmer and heightens the underwater impression, so that were a shoal of angel fish to swim in view it would scarcely be remarked upon. But the impression is purely a visual one. No one feels that they are under the sea and the feeling of stifling humidity is antagonistic to the vision and I suppose no one else sees the picture in these terms. The backs of many jackets are stained with great patches of sweat, and with no physical effort it starts between the fingers, above the eyes and stands out on the forehead in tiny transparent hemispheres. But to the left booms the sea and rushes up the beach in feathery scrolls. That is our rescue. And we live in it. The sand is so hot that you can't stand on it in bare feet, so it's into the sea at once, so very blue it is and its arching fringes so swan white and the brown black bodies of the West Kents so glistening and so dripping with sparkling drops that it is a picture that cries to be painted and might be called 'Midas bathes among his jewels', for every splash is a golden touch. Away over, left-wards, a whalelike rock noses out as though to outflank us and charge with gaping maw, and a misty town clings to its side like a flock of white gulls.

Does the scene attract you? Mebbe, but the waters of the Medway round the piers of Aylesford bridge—Ruth agreed that Wat Tyler marched over that—and on Sundays the mellow tones of the organ float from the church and waft through the rookeries. The cherry trees bow to the weight of their harvest and sparkling pints of Style and Winch slake the honest throats of Kentishmen and the no less honest throats of the Men of Kent. That's the scene I treasure even though the pints may cost 1s. 2d.

D   49

Of nights here we are greased and netted against the malarial mosquito—we are glamorous in swathes of white netting— but we need protection against the malarial rumour, too, for he swarms with more ubiquity than any breed of mosquito. Little West Kent, what now? If a battalion representative followed every rumour there would be no two of them to- gether and some of us would be called upon for duty at two places, for speculating tongues have consigned us to every place from January the 1st to Dawson City. And, wistfully, to within 24 hours' pass distance from home. But someone, somewhere, will take a tiny flag from a large map—poise it a moment while the breath of the division halts—and impinge it—where? On that rests whether the air will be thick with West Kent curses or my tears of joyful reunion will tumble down your back. Oh, little man with the red-banded hat, that pin you hold is every West Kent's destiny and the prayers of a thousand wives pull it westwards to the screaming cranes of an English dockside, the coughing fogs of London, black- out and the slamming of doors on piddle-smelling Paddington, the rough touch of Kentish bark or Scottish granite. You can- not dismiss it lightly yet I suspect that when the door opens and a cup of tea comes rattling in you will toss it aside and there, where it falls, go we.

Tomorrow I will write you again though Frank Robinson warns me that you will be seeing so much of the postman that I won't stand a chance.

8.8.'43

This will be a dull letter because that's how I feel today. So dull in fact that I didn't write any more that day. But today the weather is much better for in spite of a high wind from which there is no sheltering, there's a great slab of grey cloud across the sky, and that's lovely. The sea has lost its temper and is thrashing about all over the shore, but the cool break is very welcome.

Lately we've had Post-War plans, discussions on Art and nothing of what's on at the moment in our letters. Let's alter that today. Yesterday we had our first taste of the sirocco. I was in town at Italian class and the sweat was dripping from us, arms, forehead and even at such unlikely places as the kneecaps. We sweltered through the lesson. Then we went into the native quarter to buy some grapes—12 francs a kilo (2½ lb. a bob!). Then a gust came down the market. Any greenery, you thought, would shrivel like potato crisps. It was stifling. It was just like standing in front of a terrific exhaust pipe—as hot as that. But at the camp things were more exciting. Apparently the worst happened while we were in the Italian class and all we felt in the market was a weak flip of the sirocco's tail. At camp, they told me, a terrific hot, thick sandstorm came with it. They choked and groped. Tents were flying in the air, and, showing a complete indifference to rank, the sergeants' mess was attacked. Dinner meal was on and the tables were upset and food dropped on to the sand. The poles of the marquee were uprooted and the place saved from disaster only by the prompt action of the mess waiters who clung desperately, each to a pole. One half collapsed and all the boys—between the blinding gusts— were 'rooting' for the wind versus sergeants. 'Let it go,' they shouted to the mess orderlies. 'Let it go.' Other ranks' food was being served in the open and between the brief lulls lids were whipped off and 'muckos' slapped the food into the

51

mess tins. Then whee-ee, up came the sirocco again and swamped it with sand. Meanwhile another marquee had collapsed, the cookhouse was flattened and a million papers sent swirling out to sea. Fortunately my hatches had been securely battened down and nothing was lost from my tent. It seems that a good time was had by all. We have long been accustomed to wind devils—little whirlpools of sand that travel in swift and growing spirals throughout the camp. Everybody laughs at the discomfort of those caught in its path, but their expression often changes suddenly as the wind devil changes its course and swoops down on the wrong tents. It carries papers high aloft and I'm afraid that somewhere in Africa there is more than one original Robson waiting to be picked up.

15.8.'43

I have eaten, so now's the time to talk, pull up your chair, you that side and me this. What's to talk about? Well, I never did tell you about Constantine did I? Constantine was a place that simply took my breath away, and mebbe that's why I didn't tell you about it before. It's the place where I told you we might live for a time and sit and watch the teeming life below. If the balconies are of wrought iron, which I am inclined to doubt, Constantine at one period must have had blacksmiths like our old-time village smiths, every one a craftsman, shoeing a horse, fashioning a ploughshare and executing an intricate altar screen, all with equal ease. These balconies have, most of them, involved, fascinating and rare patterns. All the way down the street and all the way up the front of the building, many stories high, the people sit in much the same way as in England they stand at front gates, the main difference being that whereas the French will knit, the English only natter. You would have found great delight in all this and my own enjoyment was enhanced by thinking of what your reactions would be to it all. The life is different from peacetime conditions with the substitution of varied soldiery for varied tourists. Yanks, our boys, Spahis, Arabs and French, with the inevitable long loaves like a rugger ball tucked tightly under one arm.

I was yanked out of that chair with about as much ceremony as you would expect from a press-gang. It is now two days later and I haven't had time to pause let alone get back to that chair. But you'll be pleased to hear that the target for the Burnett fund was reached and passed and when it all comes in it will be nearer to seventy than fifty pounds. Great stuff! But this will be the first you've heard of it. I send you the 'all about it' in a green envelope but they dilly and dally and will probably be overtaken by this. From it developed a Battalion Casualty Fund for the forming of which a meeting was held on Sunday. I was elected chairman. This fund will result in a much more live battalion, for to raise money there will be shooting matches, inter-platoon football games, quizzes, spelling bees and I know not what else. We may even have a gymkhana with melon-shies, donkey derbies, relay races, throwing the discus, swinging the lead, and so on. All of which you will agree are splendid things for combating the deadly browned-offness. In connection with this fund there are letters to write, minutes to compile and no end of dodging about. In addition to which I have been shifted from one long-houred job to one on the water care, which though interesting and verree-verree responsible (if I yielded to the temptation of putting hops into the tank there's no telling what complaints the battalion would go down with) demands even longer hours. This is the first letter home I've written for a week and it's not surprising. . . .

1.9.'43

. . . Several band instruments have arrived here lately. Good, we will form a band. Who can play? No one? Then we will teach them. And at night, on the fringe of the water the more considerate would-be musicians can be seen blowing across the ocean, very shaky, very uncertain, very tremolo. Andrew is learning the double bass bombarda, whatever that is. I haven't seen it yet, but he says it's like holding a very fat brass baby. Even now a cornet is dreaming of a white Christmas with long, dying-out notes, gasps, ejections of breath and nerve-racking pauses which keep us in a state of apprehensive suspense. The cornet struggled halfway through 'Solitude', struck a wrong note and a concerted wince went along the tables of the rest-room here. The player is going a fair way to getting his solitude.

I wasn't there myself owing to a slight touch of the sun but there was a huge fire yesterday which needed three battalions to get it under control. Trees and grass crackled fiercely I'm told and the flames showed an alarming tendency to throw out flaming pincers which moved at great speed, cutting fellows off time and again. Fortunately they all succeeded in breaking through, but it was certainly no picnic. Chaps with smouldering boots were continually scrambling down to the stream to immerse them.

54

10.9.'43

With all the A.A. Gunners of the Red Army making a bee-line for Moscow to fire victory salvoes, with half their factories given over to the production of blanks for the said salvoes—with the invasion of Italy, the probable release of my brother Ben, the imminence of further invasions, these are indeed great days. The going home chart has attained a new high and Scruff Barton says will you and I go round his place for Christmas. I warned him against being too optimistic and said Boxing Day, and will we be having a Turkey. Persia has come in now and it is expected that jeeps will be replaced by the famous magic carpets and if my squadron doesn't alight at Edgware pretty soon our thinking has all been wishful.

Where were you and what were you doing on Saturday the 4th. I was thinking of you a lot and picturing how you'd have enjoyed being with me. In the local harbour we held a very successful swimming gala. Plying leisurely limbs through pellucid waters we could see, way below us, rocks and all varieties of fish, some brightly barred and sizeable. There are octopus in the harbour too, I've seen a row of eight of them for sale in the market, about the size of a wicker shopping basket, but we encountered none that day. I competed in the naval engagement and boat race, rubber dinghies. In the boat race we came a gallant last due mainly to Percy Ross making most of the journey on his back in the well of the boat, his feet gesticulating like an upturned octopus and Robinson giving such terrific pulls on his oar as to send the boat spinning. Then again on arriving at the starting point we found we had so much water in our craft that we all leapt into the water and inverted it to clear it out. But we made such a bother about climbing in again that it took more water than it had before. Then Percy, in order to bale out, planked his bottom on the extreme edge of the raft, with the result that that side was completely under water. Otherwise, of course, we would have won. In the naval engagement there was a short, sharp encounter. Their 'torpedo', a swimmer, was deadly, and in a short time we were bobbing about in the water again. I am putting in for survivor's leave! The final winner of this event was the C.O. He was good. Altogether, it was an excellent setting, the predominant colours—orange and red. It was good to see Chopper in the water, brown body gleaming and yellow hair streaming like a mermaid's behind him. He's a porpoise in the water, flashing and sparkling all around, I often wish I could pin it to canvas.

Every cut we get here usually turns septic. Dozens of chaps have bandaged limbs. Myself, I chipped a knee on a rock in the harbour and that's gone the same way. Painful, and I playing football this evening. But our blankets are never without their quota of sand so perhaps that is the cause. You'll have to sleep in the other bed when I come home for without a couple of shovelsful of sand in the bed I shall not sleep. Likewise you must put a handful of sand in the spuds and allow me to put my mess tin, mug, boots, slippers and so on carefully on the folded blankets with mug handle pointing invariably to the right.

The newly formed band is blasting away with pumpkin cheeks, with little mercy and less musical acumen.

The other night the radio gave us the news of the fall of Stalingrad. Ah! That night we stretched on the sand by the radio, there was a half moon and the cigarettes glowed and we all wondered what you were doing at home, how glad you'd be—how many pints were being swallowed and hang the one and twopence. I was rushing down the road with you —just being impossibly happy as I always am when I'm with you. Oh, lovely wife, what a homecoming that will be. I'm sure I won't talk much. I'll be content to look and touch things. Such a great coming back it will be. But I can't go on in this vein in the public part of the air letter, though when I get back I'll have no misgivings at all. I shall kiss you loud and long in the middle of the road and to blazes with the hooting traffic and querulous drivers. Though the atmosphere will be such that no driver will be querulous at all—cor luv us no, they'll smile beatific smiles, sigh gusty sighs, switch off their engines, place their elbows on the wheel and murmur: 'Ah me, it's worth going overseas—a reception like that!' Gosh, how impatient I am to push the clock round. Meantime love to everybody and to you fair spouse, another salvo not blanks this time, but a full salvo of eloquent swallows, our own emissaries who speak with the voice of music, poetry and— well, they'll tell you I kinda like you.

21.9.'43

Billy Buffin says give him two battalions of pikemen and a company of archers and he'll clear Italy in a week. So I gives him the go-ahead and I still sees him kicking around next day and says: 'How come?' 'Well,' he says, 'the cooks wouldn't give us no haversack rations and we sticks out for our rights and we ain't going till we get 'em, Sire.' Chopper's just come in with a yarn that the M.O., being so impressed with a smart salute he gave him, that he stopped and inquired if he—

Chopper—had any social background. Vacancies in the O.C.T.U. apparently. Another Chopper story turned on the Divisional swimming finals. Dick Garratt won the 100 yards and against a Division that's no mean feat, yet for a prize he was awarded three bottles of beer! 'Picture Dick in Civvy Street,' Chopper says, 'telling someone he'd won the Divisional final. "Garn, you didn't do no such thing," the someone says. "O.K." Dick will say. "Come round to my place and I'll prove it, I'll show you the empty beer bottles!"'

At the moment, Duckie, I am conducting some secret experiments. At midnight the moon watches me measuring drops into slender glass and it gleams greenly on phials and test tubes. In case my experiments succeed I want you to promise to handle all parcels that you get with extreme care because you may receive a small one that contains dehydrated husband and I dare say I shall be pretty bruised as it is. All you have to do is to sprinkle me with a water can, and from a little Tom Thumb man perched on your pretty toe I shall grow until I am full size again.

One of our babies has grown to strapping size and its fame has spread. The Brains Trust. Last week the Brigadier sat on it. Quite good. As he is Irish he got plenty of Irish questions. He well said: 'Very few Irishmen understand the Irish question and I think it can be said that not one Englishman does.' I don't, for everything I've read on it presupposes some preliminary knowledge and little has been clear to me.

The mountain that I can see from here looks like a volcano at the moment. A large slow plume of smoke is drifting at right angles away from the peak and since it is some twenty miles away the flame licking up one slope must be half a mile in length. Another forest fire and several of the lads have been out all night trying to cope with it. Not very successful, obviously.

30.9.'43

Today, my love, there were sports—fellows running from one place to another as fast as possible, though why I can't make out, since one place in this depressing country is just as cheerless as the next. It reminds me rather of goldfish swimming around in a bowl. It's wet wherever they go. I, lass, was meant for more dignified pursuits. I'm not a runner bean, not even a runner has-been. I'm a runner never-was. This usually results in my being run out when I play cricket. I find my partner completing his second while I am turning round at the end of the first and there we are with two batsmen at one end. So I didn't enter any races. Nor did I put the weight when I found out it did not mean putting the weight on the stomach! And of course, I who can scarely throw a shadow, could hardly be expected to throw the javelin. But I did compete in the tug-of-war. But the other side had someone pulling strings—eight Tony Gallentos to be precise—and we were somewhat ingloriously defeated. After that, with an eye to perhaps another post-war vocation, I opened a book in aid of the Battalion Casualty Fund—a fat capitalist occupation. Unfortunately they placed a guard at the gates of the stadium and I couldn't make a getaway. Didn't do too badly, so perhaps if you would keep your eyes open for a nice grey bowler, sporty with a curly brim, stridently checked suit and a horse-shoe tie-pin, I might go into the business seriously when I come home. You once told me that you and Vivi were thinking of taking up riding—you'll have plenty of opportunity. Ascot,

Goodwood, Haydock Park, and Pontefract, Cheltenham, Epsom, Sandown Park and Aintree. You'd be really horsey after all those with legs looking like a perfect pincer movement.

There was something English about the day. After the severe rains of the days previously there was a breeze, plenty of sun and lovely white clouds ambling across the sky all day and looking really paintworthy among the yellow peaks. The houses up the slope in terraced blocks, some pink and some blue, distemper shades, looked fine too.

Two lovely letters from you today, the one a continuation of the other and I am vastly placated, I will deal with them tomorrow. I must leave you now, a thing I shall never do once I am home. We'll be handcuffed together to make sure. Good night.

1.10.'43

Today the foreground of our picture is streaked with long leaden puddles. The rains are here in earnest. Sudden squalls, tents billow, noisy with wind, slapping and booming. The tight rein of the guys is not always proof when the mettlesome beast has the bit between his teeth. The rain hisses and seethes imperiously on the tent top. Sounds of a desperate mallet whacking pegs can be heard from all sides. And I am pretty sure that Paddy was only too correct when he said: 'What are we moaning for, worse is to come!' Paddy is a droll pessimist. The Mediterranean is in masterful mood, its sunny and blue days defeated. It's a churning tormented element of frightening power. Its colours are ugly, it throws a very good spume. The background for terrible events. It rushes up the shore dangerously close to our tents. We won't retreat. We are silly, silly and brave and no doubt someone is going to do a desperate Canute in the dark as the sea rushes through the camp. Or will the guard keep it in check. They're armed with tommy guns you know, and they aren't to be despised.

There are some curious birds wheeling over the water. I should say they were swifts from the scimitar sweep of their wings, but there is a white bar down their cheeks which baffles me. They tumble and dart after the butterflies, for, if you please, butterflies have chosen such a moment to descend upon us. True they came yesterday when there were bright intervals but though much reduced in numbers they are still in evidence today. They came by the thousand, like handfuls of confetti they fluttered from the sea—or like the advance flakes of a snowstorm, in such unbelievable numbers. It's possible that they have brought the birds. The boys are digging out their thicker clothing for the atmosphere has a Scottish chill about it and my fingers were none too warm this morning. Harry, who is sitting next to me, thinks it's 'bloody cold, Robbie'. It sure is. Could do with a fireside talk now, but you're dressmaking and I'd sit on the scissors and your mouthful of pins doesn't make for easy conversation. I guess it's a pretty sight all the same and there's something appetizing on the stove. I can smell it. Your mother praises your cooking. I am not in a position to do that unfortunately, but I praise the effort heartily. Are you good at bread pud-dings and duffs? That's all I demand of you. But carry on the good work. There is a horrible example of culinary casualness within the family. My Uncle Bob was a healthy sailor once, he was rubicund and ruddy. He thumped people on the backs roaring a stentorian 'Belay there, my hearty!' He rollicked. All through the last war he'd run against no rocks, was in no wrecks. Three weeks married to my redoubtable Aunt Alice he encountered rock cakes and divers other questionable concoctions. He was a wreck from then on. 'He carries all the burdens of the world upon his shoulders,' people say. And indeed it looks it. Where before he was jaunty, he now droops, no more the romping terrier but a down-in-the-mouth snarler, belching continually. My Aunt Alice cannot cook, but will try. Practice never made my Aunt Alice perfect. Her cooking would kill an ostrich and clog a concrete mixer. So, please, Margaret, my love, treat this matter of cooking with all seriousness. It's like the show business. To give delight entails hard work. The light approach means ponderous pastry. Approximate only halfway to Sofia, attain an apple tart but half as appetizing as hers and I promise I'll come home to you. Try? Good.

14.10.'43

The worst storm I've known last night. Burst quite suddenly and the sergeants' mess, the marquee in which Chopper and I sleep, became a battered ship on the furious deep and in a trice I was Fletcher Christian and Chopper Captain Bligh, though Capn. Bligh's behaviour halfway up the pole while the tent was suddenly dark and vivid with lightning, and screaming above the wind 'Save the rum, Mr. Christian,' was hardly consistent with his rank. Oscar Wynne was in the tent too, battening down hatches, lashing the wheel and all the rest of it, while the tent caved in one side and threatened to flounder any moment. The side pegs were torn up and the sides flapped vigorously as though the tent were trying to take off. And there was the flashing of the lightning, the rolling of the thunder and the tremendous drumming of the rain, fierce as bullets, and we three enacting the drama of the high seas.

But even gone with the wind has an ending, and after half an hour or so of this we put the tables in the centre and went to sleep underneath them. These storms and irresistible winds occur with greater frequency now and a large part of the week is occupied in re-erecting tents. In this wind they go up and down like pack-o'-card towns. Grand exhibition this morning. A piano was sent for a concert, and as the tent it was in was blown down, it was shifted to the main dining hall. Hermy got on it at breakfast time, began thumping and it started. A rip-roaring sing song at the breakfast tables! Blokes bunging Spam into their mouths and roaring 'Mary' at the same time, the whole tent and every table. You never saw such a sight in your life and very soon Hermy didn't lack for accompaniment for Skinner, Sailor Haines and Bob Langridge came to the piano with spoons and began to rattle them castanet fashion. It was a glorious picture and I'll draw it for you.

There is a large moon tonight, and a wide silver sheen on the sea. Occasionally a frieze is formed by figures passing in silhouette. There is a faint mist that presages a frost. The night sky is a grey blue, the sea a deeper shade of the same leaden hue. The hills are wrapped in softening mist and moonlight. The sea sighs. So do I!

28.11.'43

Today, chicken at l'Hotel d'Orient with Andrew, Stan,

Khallif, Mosah and Nur Ed Din, all of which are no doubt
wrongly spelt and deficient of a few accents. Mosah's name
means Moses and Nur Ed Din's the Flower of Religion, in
this case no exotic orchid bloom. It is Sunday, the walk
through the tree-lined streets in the inconstant sun very
pleasant and not unmindful of an English Sunday morning.
Why? There were soldiers, sailors, and shoeshine boys and
occasionally a female. It was the leisurely, go-to-church air,
the same spaciousness that our Sunday has.

I am bad at languages and the phrase books are silly. We
met our friends in the Glacier Café and what could I say to
really impress them? Wet my fingers and flick the pages over.
Oh dear! 'This is my Grandpere,' but Andrew isn't, nor is
Stan. And the Arabs wouldn't want to meet him anyway.
'Embrace me, ma chérie.' No, Khallif, even though I have
an affection for you, my wife might object. Ah! but here was
one: 'Voulez-vous boire un apéritif avec moi?' And that
cost me drinks all round. A little knowledge is certainly dangerous.

After dinner we strolled again. Here and there we passed a
bombed house, white sides fallen like a landslide and thousands of tiles exposed. There are always thousands of tiles in
these houses, floors, walls, and everything that is tileable.

It will not have escaped the notice of my vigilant spouse
that it is only to Khallif that we talk. Alas, he is the only one
that speaks English and to the Flower of Religion and Mosah
we can only smile. We smile at each other quite a lot. Rather
silly but they know what we mean. Smiling, like music, love
and war, is universal. Then the Flower dashes off somewhere
and returns with a key which he puts in a keyhole, the
Flower's house perhaps? But it is used as a store rather. There

are bales here and straw in another room and in the courtyard
a ram standing on wet straw like varnish. He will be killed in
a fortnight, explained Khallif, to commemorate the Abraham
and Isaac sacrifice. But he is a good fighter and he explains
also that rams are kept for that purpose here and that there
are town championships.

2.12.'43

I went to Navy House for a debate the other night but
was a day early. So I became Cassius in the play reading.
That's the first play reading I've ever done, and in Cassius,
upon whom the first two acts hinge, I had a fat part. Gielgud
had to put in a few years as a props-boy before he got the
part of the third Citizen. But there was I wheedling and in-
sinuating and sapping the good resolves of our Brutus in a
trice. Some have fame thrust upon them. 'He strides the
world like a Colossus while we petty men peer and scrape
between his legs.' I'm not sure that's quite right but that's
where Gielgud and I differ again. He remembers all the words
all the way through. So does Olivier; so did Garrick, Kean
and Kemble. Thus Shakespeare hasn't developed any. The
great artist doesn't give a hoot for the words, he goes on
playing as he thinks. This gives him more time to devote to
acting as he doesn't have to spend hours swotting and remembering—and moreover when he plays he plays to packed
houses, for clearly his performance is never hackneyed, is
more individual, has more facets and nuances since it isn't
limited by boundaries set by the Author. I shall never forget
the blustering applause of the audience at Dallas Hippodrome
when a famous actor playing Mark Antony declaimed:

E   65

'Friends, Romans, Countrymen, here are the baseball results.'
You see, there's true art there and in a twinkling he had
included the audience in the play and they were checking
their pools at once. They do those things so much better in
America.

I've been working at the theatre this last week, painting
scenery. Very congenial. But not without difficulties in the
way of materials. The canvas is rather long in the tooth, with
rents here and there, but brushes and colour are the chief lack.
All have to be scrounged, so we have camouflage paint, oil
paint, distemper, and water paint to play with, not much of
any and already we have had to make innovations. Thus we
have used blanco and dissolved mepacrine tablets which
produce a makeshift yellow. In the matter of brushes it is
worse still. I have an old inch brush in such an advanced stage
of dandruff it won't last long, and two decrepit brushes of the
type that go with Willie's first water-colour outfit. Very
small so that our scenery is going to be done in line and
pointillist technique. Imagine it—a *pointillist* backcloth . . .

In the summer one of the boys sent home for some lemon-
ade crystals. They arrived today when everybody is huddled
up and goose-pimpled and sneezing, coughing and cursing
the geography books for not even breathing a word about
this.

4.12.'43

. . . I am a 'P.V.O.'. What does that mean? That means
patient under observation. I am in hospital and tickled pink.
They don't know what I've got, but apart from a blitzing
cough I don't feel bad, not ill at all, just pleasantly unwell,

enjoying the highest degree of luxury since I've been out here. And as I say, tickled pink, wearing pyjamas and sketching, smiling comfortably into the corrugated vault of the Nissen hut marked 'Wimbledon', which is my ward. No buxom females for nurses, I'm afraid, but I'd have to be on my best behaviour if there were any women here. My temperature baffles them, creating a chart that reads rapid slumps and booms, and they listen with stethoscopes for the underground movement. But there's solidarity among my corpuscles and nary a quisling comes forward to blow the gaff. I did a very cold and miserable guard the morning before I reported sick, even then I didn't report sick, just dropped in to try my temperature and was bunged into bed forthwith. Of course I could tell 'em what it is—but you'd think they'd be able to tell homesickness when they see it, wouldn't you?

9.12.'43

I have an agreeable arrangement with my temperature, it is this: When I am up it climbs and when I go to bed it subsides. Thus, after being in hospital for a week, and being allowed to return to the unit, I was back again the very next morning with the same unknown malady and a temperature of 101. Now, in bed again, it is almost normal and I wade through the books I have been meaning to read at nineteen to the dozen. My hair at the back is developing waves from pressure against the corrugated walls as I write. In short, culture has a chance, and I am not unhappy. Except in as much as I have this one air-letter and several people who expect to hear from me before Christmas. This will be impossible now and I will ask you to make apologies for me. The oils

and the Italian arrived the same day and a beautiful letter of
the Christmas scene in our domestic future. And, as you say,
the next Christmas is our one. Meanwhile, there is this
Christmas. Give my greetings to everybody. Make it as enjoyable as possible. And now join me in looking at our Christmas of the future. The snow is drifting down silently, and
the roof is like icing on a cake, there are bells in the distance,
soft curling blue smoke, and you look like an Eskimo beside
me, with your fur gloves, thick coat, and head shawl. The
snow settles on your nose and on your hair it is like dew on
a web. Your cheeks are flushed with the enjoyment of the
evening and your eyes sparkle with pleasure over an armful
of presents. That red glow marks our little cottage, you can
smell its warmth from here. I drop one parcel, and snow-
covered and bedraggled, out of nowhere it seems, a plump
comical black dog appears, to stuff his nose into my ear as I
try to pick the parcel up. He is lost. Let's take him home,
you say. And so we do and then your story begins.

26.1.'44

You've read all the stories about the stage stars in the front
line I suppose, and probably think your old man lies back in
a deck-chair to be twanged at by Formby, emoted at by
Viviene Leigh, and stripped at by Dixie Lee. You're hopelessly wrong, Duckie. They came to Africa, but never to the
hinterland where the majority of the troops are. But we have
a cinema here, a profit-making shell, the minimum for the
maximum. The films are taken out of mummy wrappings
and the actors perform in the torrential rain which marks
the antediluvian film. They are cut so that the film is often

episodic and very often impossible to follow and the sound is like an Edison original through a very tinny horn. The place itself is huge, wooden chairs and a vast roof of unique quality, it is composed of inverted carpets! Funny. And Buffin the bizarre digs me with his elbow and says: 'I'm glad you're not one of those silly *humans* dear—you'd be falling right down there by now.' He's always in some other world, Buffin. And he doesn't read a book so much as learn it in so many parts. Norah sent him *Caravan* the other day. So all this week I am referred to as 'Pablo', and several times Guiseppe Buffin (Lance-Corporal) has tried to sell me a dancing bear. 'Och, my chevvy chal! The wild wicked music and the crash of gipsy tambourines! 'Tis the life.'

Have just been notified that we can tell of our change of address. Now M.E.F., which does not mean Italy, but does explain your shortage of mail. I'm afraid you never really appreciate the conditions. There's no coming into a room you know, with chairs, table and electric light. Letters are written prone on the floor, which is sand—by hurricane lamp or candlelight—with several chaps trying to use it, casting shadows and heaven knows what. Now we don't half know long nights for it is dark by six. Just consider that alone; candles from six, and often no candles at all. Perhaps there's been one candle but you can't write by candle unless it's alongside your ear, so it's been to bed and discussions.

8.2.'44

I have been to Cairo! Forty-eight hours' leave. But I didn't see the Pyramids, nor the Sphinx. Everyone gasps and says: 'What, you didn't?' incredulous like. I didn't want to much.

I had chicken dinners, a Turkish bath and did three cinema shows with Billy Buffin and Bob Langridge. Cairo is like London. Buildings, streets and tramcars and big and breakneck. I am a plough jockey by nature and I don't take kindly to cities. Not that I didn't welcome the leave. I did. The hotel was armified but sheets and a bed and wash basins were a welcome reach back into the past; and if shoeshine boys came into your room in the early morning, and a newspaper seller and a guide to the pyramids, well, tea in bed and a white ceiling to look up to made those things tolerable.

Cairo has plenty of everything, but what isn't too expensive is terribly shoddy. It has thousands of aggressive street vendors of all types and shoeshine boys of all sizes who try to bully folk into custom by rudeness, persistence and weight of numbers—for they throw cordons round you and if you refuse they tip a nice blob of blacking, which here is the consistency of jam, on their brush and threaten to throw it over you. I saw a knife pulled on one; and two Black Watch fellows go lickety-split down two streets in pursuit of another. It was not surprising.

1944

ITALY

In Cairo with Buffin I saw a newsreel showing our boys in Italy. You've seen similar films I expect. I saw mule-teams toiling up the snowy heights and I shuddered. Then we had letters from Robinson, Redwood and Harry Millward. These last two had been in the line for several weeks and eventually came out of it sick, with fatigue more than anything else I think. Well, I'm not sure how much of it we can say, but we're in Italy. We landed at the beautiful port of 'Hush-hush', staggered off the ship tremendously laden with packs and two kit-bags. To land we had to scramble across the wreck of a bombed ship, its funnel broken and pointing out like an extra gun. There were Italian men begging for food and scrambling for any morsel thrown to them. The town was hollow and echoed like a city of the dead. Rubble intestines of lovely buildings were tumbled on to the pavement. Bombing and shelling had obviously been pretty thick. My view of Italy from that moment to the spot where I am now was the severely circumscribed one offered from the interior of a crowded truck. But it was good to see trees again and quite a few of them. We went on and on, and climbed and climbed up into the snow. The moon was on the snow and it looked good but it was a sharp and disconcerting change from the Egyptian desert. De-bus and a mile or so of marching to a village, and into billets. Ours was a sort of wine vault, for it held grinding and grape-crushing machinery, with a spout for the juice. The hurricane lamp threw more shadows than light, but we groped down to sleep on the floor, Hicky, Chopper, Buffin, Hermy and the rest.

Italy, as I was soon to discover, is a mixture of Devon, Cornwall and the Scottish Highlands, all steep, surprising and beautiful, with quaintness here in the villages, and grandeur above where shines the snow. Spring flowers sparkle everywhere, and noisy streams tumble over the boulders. Whereas in Scotland men will stand in them tempting the trout, here women stand in them, bent over their washing, and whacking it on rocks. The land seems rich enough, and eager with the surge of spring, but however responsive it is, it cannot satisfy the people who patiently till it. What a long preparation for a meal! The hoe that scrapes in the spring gets a reward, when? Summer at the earliest, and for the most part, autumn. A long time to wait for a hungry people. And they are hungry. How much so it is difficult to tell, probably varies in different parts. But certainly no one is well fed, and it is said that a woman will sell herself for a tin of corned beef. That is joked about, but underneath the fellows are filled with the great pity of it. And our group at least slips food furtively to the civilians, but in view of the stories, feel awkward when giving it to the women. They usually press it on them and dash away, followed by voluble and touching 'gratios'. We feed in the village street. Not very considerate to a hungry village folk, or to the chaps who have to feed before their gaze. There's no way out of this, for lack of a hall. The kids are usually scraping into jam tins, and if the army is billeted in their village they do all right. But how the older folk fare I cannot say, nor has there been any chance to find out.

The village we were in was a delight from the drawing point of view. They all are. Cobbled, with arches, picture doorways and natty corners, unexpected and a joyful jumble. Then there are donkeys mincing along the cobbles, goats, sheep, and women bearing earthenware pitchers on their heads. Why the livestock still live puzzles me, unless these are the minimum required for breeding.

Our billet has an underground atmosphere and as usual there was all the old play acting. Buffin fancies himself as some Capulet with doublet and hose, and in the street tests an imaginary rapier, bending it and weighing it in his hands. Then Capulet is gone and Tito is the part. We all have leather jerkins and cap comforters (scarves which make the most comfortable head-wear in the army) and so we look the part. 'A sight for sore Italian eyes.' Lots of kids had sores and chilblains (barefooted some of the kids) and we had them round the fire bathing and bandaging them.

14.3.'44

A place in Surrey? Sure. Any place out of London suits me. London's O.K. for peeping into now and again but no more than that for me, thank you. I've got a nice little place here at the moment, sharing it with Arthur Stevens. A bijou flat, perhaps just a little too bijou, for we couldn't swing many cats in it even if (a) we had the cats, and (b) we wanted to swing the dear little things. It is made of rock, very airy, with a roof of branches and canvas. We cannot kneel to make the bed but have to lie on one side to do it. Low timbered roofs are all very well in Kent and the Cotswolds but it is my firm opinion that here ye olde worlde stuff is carried a bit too far, or too low. It's like sleeping in the drawer of the kitchen table. We wriggle in or out according to whichever way we are going. One of the biggest advantages is that we are never troubled by people selling vacuum cleaners. The absence of these slick gentry is probably due to our neighbour across the way—a blue-eyed Aryan who keeps popping brickbats down a mortar barrel and slinging them over to us. A low practice, and I think I'd sooner live in Tottenham. That is distinctly high-toned compared to this district. Similar structures to ours go all the way down the slope—regular ribbon development. Arthur, looking at the view, is murmuring: 'My God, if I took a photo of that in technicolor people would never believe it.'

The distant peaks, snow-topped, are pink in the light of the setting sun. Villages hold on to the slopes somehow and look like nothing more than clutches of partridge eggs. The day, after the miserable rain of yesterday, has been radiant, but last night, burr—talk about night on the bare mountain. The wind ripped up the slope and snorted through the many gaps in the walls till even my heart, for all its warmth for Margaret Gunn, was well-nigh frostbitten.

Some of the climbs here are terrific, and we're always heavily laden with extras, such as blankets, because we know we're going to need them when we get up top. We, the S.B.s, have what they call alpine packs, huge things on an iron hip frame. Besides this, I have so many things slung round my neck that if—as I devoutly wish—I could stand in the middle of a village green in England on May Day, I'd make a perfect maypole. With all that weighty paraphernalia we have to climb mountains with a stretcher. And you tell me we'll holiday in the Hebrides! If they fit escalators we will! Climbing in the mud is nice and soppy. At times a hand and knee scramble while we often find a previous spurt nullified, as we sometimes slip back. What it was like in the winter I cannot imagine, a whole-time nightmare I should say. But now the sun is beginning to prevail, and apart from the Mrs. Grundying of hostile mortars, there is, as there was in the earlier Tunis days, quite a holiday atmosphere about things. Food, if a little monotonous, is plentiful. There is more chocolate than we can manage, enough fags, and yesterday a welcome distribution of comforts knitted back home, socks and two-piece scarves with hood. Very ducky. Supplies come up by mule trains, led either by Sikhs, or Italian mountain troops who have a most fetching number in hats, not unlike Peter Pan's with a lovely long rakish feather. Must get one of those, girl.

Last year Frank Robinson had a birthday in the line. 'Here's another present for me,' he'd say as another shell whined and he ducked into the ditch. Now in two days' time it's my turn. They'll come over with ribbons, I expect: 'Happy birthday to you. Happy birthday to you!'

19.3.'44

Fairest Spouse,

A guy scrambled blindly down the slope, whimpering: 'Hullo—what's up?' Steve and I crawled out of our sangar. There was the chap, tin hat, overcoat, leather jerkin, bala-clava, all muffled up, but shivering and sobbing that he couldn't stand it. Machine-guns had been stuttering starkly up top of two hills, and these new kids feel it occasionally, though most of them are good. 'Come on, kid, you'll be O.K.' and we scrambled down to the advanced dressing station across the valley. In the reassuring light of this place (a well-made, much larger stand-up-in-able sangar of one large room and two ante-rooms) we gave him a cigarette and hot tea. He didn't drink much but sat shivering with two tears crawling down his nose. A doctor felt his pulse and we left him.

Getting back was a nightmare. We held hands because, were we a foot apart, we could not have seen each other, and this was the only way we could keep contact. So there we were, blind and tumbling about the rocks, holding hands. We wondered what Margaret Gunn and Jean would have said if they could have seen us. Sangars with canvas roofs are tucked neatly into the slopes and we were never sure that we weren't stepping into one. There would have been such a crash and skirmish had we done so. And we talked loudly for the benefit of the sentries who, blind as we were, might fire at anything sounding too quiet and creepy. We got tangled up with 'phone wires, climbed over boulders which on a normal night we could have worked round, knocked over a tin of water, and finished the journey on hands and knees. All the time it was raining. Eventually we got back to our blankets and shivered all night. We had all our clothes on, and our warm leather jerkins (we haven't had our clothes off for a week), but just the same, we shivered. And can you wonder at it? Of course you can't. For the next morning everything was white. A thick fall of snow. Oh, darling, and back in the village, in our kit-bags, we still had our tropical shorts. 'What a birthday,' I said, for it was March 16th. We shivered and shivered. And the blue-eyed Aryan over the way popped a few presents over. Nice of him, but the others considered it a trifle anti-social. But there's fun too among all this, and soon the hill side was ringing with 'It was a lover and his lass', a lovable thing which I am very fond of, and which started being popular on the ship coming across. 'With a hey and a ho and a hey.' I'd sing from the bottom of the slope; my namesake

Capt. R. would reply: 'With a hey and a ho nonny nonny no.' He sings Spanish war songs, too, and yesterday went through Shostahovitch's 'Salute to Life'.

During action we S.B.s are split up and attached to companies. That's what we don't like. There's four to a company, and it means that our lovable characters are deployed. Hermy and Chopper with 'A', Hicky with 'B', Buffin with 'D', while Steve and myself with Tony Marchant and Jimmy Bint are with 'C'—which in Tunis was captured entire, and recovered again at the final crash. There's a terrific bond between all these I've mentioned. When 'A' or 'B's' position is under fire it's always our S.B.s there we first think of. We won't see each other all together again until we go back out of the line.

We had a dodgy job the other night. A chap was wounded on patrol, out in no-man's-land on the top of the world with a bright moon flooding everything with light and silvering the clouds *below*. There we dressed his wounds, guarded by a Bren-gunner with chocolate smeared over his face. He was bleeding when we found him, but the patrol found movement too risky to dress him. Two leg wounds, one broken, and a stomach wound. But he was grand. 'I'll try not to moan, chaps,' he said. They are very calm sometimes, the wounded. Then followed the worst journey of that bloke's life—down the mountain on a stretcher. Sliding, climbing, stumbling over boulders, starting a dozen little avalanches. He was cold, he said, but we were sweating profusely for over half an hour before we got him to the A.D.S. Capt. Yardley was there, stubbled, heavy-eyed, boots undone, far from the polish of Sandhurst, but with a steadying effect to any wounded with his long strong face and capable hands. I think our casualty will recover, for a bullet through the stomach has a way of pushing the intestines to one side and passing through. Now worry not sweetness. The incidents I've related are the tense ones and at this stage are not representative of life out here. Frankly, I find I enjoy a lot of it—and anyway, I think the back of the job is broken. I'll be back.

27.3.'44

My beautiful Margaret Gunn,

It takes a Steinbeck to tell it. I can achieve only a faint echo, a fifth-rate narrator with a first-hand experience. That's where I have the pull. Let me try to exploit it. It is about a journey which perhaps justifies the word 'epic'. We lost one man on it. Heaven knows where, for it was dark, and the column single file: mebbe down the steep side of the ravine, mebbe in the fast-flowing river, mebbe he just subsided in his tracks and went to sleep. We don't know, for now, four days later, he is still missing. It had been over for several hours when another man collapsed from exhaustion. And we—we slept, rousing for meals, for most of forty-eight hours. Tiredness and exhaustion.

Let's begin at the beginning. Maggie Gunn's photograph lightened the wall of our sangar way up among the peaks. You have become Maggie, you see, and there were two spring flowers adorning it—though failing with the comparison. But that day it wasn't 'I'm wrinkling my nose at you, Maggie', as it had been before—from Steve and Tony too; but 'I'm crackling my icicles at you'. (Icicles on my beard, for it was bitterly cold.) The Blankshires were to relieve us at eleven o'clock. Always in the dark. Oh, but what a time they were.

Jerry hadn't started his nightly bout of shelling. We wanted to be out of it before he did. A fortnight of this was enough for anyone. In our sangar, the paper stuffed in the chinks not really effective against the draughts, we knelt in a peculiar position. Our heads to the ground and our feet drumming rapidly for warmth, something like ostriches. Miserably, miserably cold. The 24th March. My father's birthday. Wonder what Margaret Gunn's doing. We drummed our feet, shivered and sniffed. Humour came out even then. My own. Though I don't know why. 'Tony, there's a column of penguins outside; the Blankshires can't make it.' But they did make it. Hot where we were cold, heavily laden, sweating and swearing, but swearing quietly for the Boche was only just over the ridge. We handed over to the stretcher bearers, whispering such 'griff' as we knew, telling the likely extent of casualties to expect. We were the envied, we were going out. Silently we assembled, three signallers, two snipers, runners, batmen and S.B.s. Also Sergeant-major Freddie Beadle, about eighteen all told. The platoons would follow.

We started off, going gingerly over the rocks to the track. Crash! I went over. Tony bent to get my tin hat. Crash! Over he went too. Sh—silence man! Along the track following the white tape. Around the horseshoe twist in the track, above a deep ravine; look down, and by the light of the stars against the white rocks are two shapes, still shapes. Mules that have gone over the edge. Surprising that, because the path, though not easy, isn't as narrow as all that. You'd expect mules to keep it. But they are laden, and the men who drive them, French and Italian, are hard drivers. We heard later that they had lost thirty that day, though that number has probably grown with each telling. We went down, and

F

down, twisting sometimes suddenly on our behinds but
mostly on our feet, gunfire flickering behind the humps and
way over and down on the flat. At intervals a sentry would
rise from the brush to whisper a challenge and to demand a
password. A gable of a pole tent here and there, relief stretcher
bearers. These were mainly negroes, West Africans, all sorts,
and all needed because it takes seventeen hours to carry a man
out of these mountains and to hospital.

Round a hump, and below, a plain with a long silver river
idling through it, turning this way and then that way, going
on only because it had to, because some law ordains that it has
to find its own level, but reluctant about it as Shakespeare's
schoolboy. Now I hasten the story along this particular
descent because I realize I am telling you about the journey
of the night before. There have been several, none have been
easy, and I started writing of the wrong one. The journey of
the 24th, the one about which I meant to tell you, started from
this bowl the night following. There were much the same
props. The stars, the booming and the gun-flashes playing
about the horizon like electric storms. Always the going was
difficult, over rocks, or through mud. Steep winding descents,
and this time the whole battalion going single-file with us
right near the front, followed by unrecognizable forms, all
incognito by virtue of the night and known only by their
swearing and stumbling. We wound down into the stygian
mouth of a ravine here which was a sinister grimace of the
mountain, and a drop here which, deep by day, took on a
more menacing character by night. Here we would be shut
in by the mountain walls, would look up and see the stars
flurrying out like sparks above, try to see also the people
making the descent in our wake, straining the eyes and seeing

them not, knowing their presence only by the slither of rocks and stones.

It is eerie in the mountains. You are conscious of the smells, the smell of sweat, earth, garlic and mint, of the grunts and panting of the man behind you, the tapping of the staffs, the scrape of twigs of an occasional dwarf tree over a tin-hat, the jolt of boots on rock. And you can frighten yourself, too. The white rocks and stones can easily become skulls, especially when you come upon a lonely grave, mebbe three side by side, and white stones set all around. 'Poor devil, he's well out of it.' But it's not him you think of, it's his people. Jerry ranged on more than an Italian slope when he got him. He ranged on an English home as well. He launched a shell and a letter. The shell brought peace to one, the letter misery to many, a wife, a child, a mother? Yesterday it was a Jerry's grave. You thought the same thoughts. A home in Wilhelmshaven. You didn't gloat. Didn't even say that's one less. You don't hate Jerry. You just say why can't we all come to our senses and call the whole thing off.

Down, down, still down. Following the white tape. Then hell, there's wire round your feet! 'Phone cable. Mind the wire! Mind the wire! The word is whispered back. Hickey, I learned later, added wickedly 'And the "S" mines'. His humour emerged in other ways too. Sardonic stuff. 'Have your exact fare ready for when you come to the buses.' Then we met the Frenchmen. A battalion of them, in single-file like us, just where the track was at its most dangerous. We had to sway to dodge their cross-slung rifles, getting too near the edge of the ravine for our liking. They sweated, grunted, smelt strongly of garlic, and every tenth man seemed to be bald-headed with his helmet in his hand. *Beaucoup Anglaise soldat.*

Mind the wire. Mind the wire. Keep to the right. Keep to the right—right of what? A tight rope? It was tricky going. One bloke went over the edge, clutched a providential bush and was hauled up again. The last Frenchman went by—when? Arthur Stevens says an hour and forty minutes after the first one and he's not far out. The last ones were straggling, running, reeling, and the very last one sobbing. Then we heard the rush of water, had a sideways slither for a bit and were upon a road, with the C.O. complaining at a hut about the wire. Then there were still more Frenchmen making for the foot of the climb. 'Poor blighters,' I said, 'they don't know what's in for them.' Steve reminded me of those words later. There was a wide river on the left, a high cliff on our right which covered the road nicely from shelling.

31.3.'44

Lovely Margaret Gunn,

I don't want to write, I want to come home and talk. Letters are such a bottleneck. There are so many things and thoughts I want to discuss with you, neither time nor space will permit it on paper. So I don't want to write. I'll idle through this. First, I haven't had an air-letter from you for over a week and no C.M.F. ones. I must get one today. Sorry, ducky, but I'm awfully 'browned'. Why? Why? Why? I do know and I don't know.

Didn't get any further than that yesterday. And yesterday a letter came from you in pencil. Which started me off with a twinge of annoyance. I'm sorry but I can't help that. The Italian book turned up but I've had little chance to study it and less to practise it. We've had nothing more than pauses in

84

Italian villages, and are now situated well clear of everything. I've seen the Isle of Capri, Vesuvius, and Naples, but for the most part it's been a bird's-eye-view of everything I've seen. On my birthday I was up among the peaks, face to face with Jerry. You were drinking my health. It's good you didn't know where I was or you wouldn't have drunk a thing and my mother would have spent the night crying. How great a mercy indeed that we are insulated in that way—that we haven't got television sight. If we had, enjoyment and laughter would be forgotten, for there is so much tragedy simultaneous with the slightest laughter that the world would be sobered for ever. My mother, dear soul, says she feels guilty when enjoying the comfort of home and the thought of us occurs, as it nearly always does occur. We feel much the same way when being dished out with food within the hungry gaze of Italian folk.

Our thoughts and talks lately have been ugly ones. Steve and I share a little pup tent (you crawl out like rabbits. 'Won't it be lovely to walk through a door again.' Hicky that was. Even little things like that have a nostalgic aura) and just as Ann used to hold court of a Sunday, so do we in this tent. Hicky, Hermy, Buff, Chopper, Percy all wriggle in. Impossible, you'd say, and we're as close as a hand of bananas. We smoke and talk. And talk—'Shut up talking like this. We're wallowing in an orgy of self pity.' I had to say that. What produces it? Partly, mainly in fact, the feeling that you can't keep on going up these mountains and coming down again. The mortars can't always hit someone else. And one day the battalion will come down without you. You trample those thoughts down but you might as well try and trample down gas, they rise again. Producing them also are the things we read in Army newspapers. The strikes and more strikes. The Second Front would stop all that. Is it poor morale? It's not the best I know. But all these blokes will be tops when they go in again.

Funny your remarks about the war being mainly impersonal, for my last letter to Clara and Goo dealt at great length with this. On the boat I was showing photographs to Eric Daws. 'I know that fellow,' he said. It was A.G.K. in the Youth Hostel photo with Curly Roots and Marjorie. Eric was lately of the Buffs—same battalion as A.G.K. He was a massive fellow, knew hundreds of songs, lots of rollicking folk songs, and is the only person I ever met, apart from an Italian prisoner, who knew 'Figaro' from beginning to end. On the boat he was terrific, and he and I got the whole mess deck going one night on Merrie England songs, rounds of songs about frogs who lived in mills. I did a portrait of him. When he saw my beard in action he called Alvarez, a Spaniard in the Intelligence Section. 'Come, the Spanish Court is in session,' he said. I looked like a Grandee according to him. A can of water was steaming on a little wood fire, his jowl was black. He frowned and thrust it out in a comical impersonation of Mussolini. He pulled his shirt over his head and I saw the muscles of his magnificent body. He always made for where I was, for he loved discussion. He won't come again. I drew his portrait on the boat. On an Italian slope, in sight of Vesuvius, I drew his grave. I remember him on the boat deep in conversation with a very dirty Arab, asking about Arabic words. So keen to live, so keen to learn. His yellow desert steel helmet was on his grave. So individual. It was him. It was the only one in the battalion. He was in an outpost and fired upon. A rock fell and crushed him. Had

86

Heinrich known what a grand fellow Eric was he would never have fired the shot that killed him. War is too impersonal. Mie was very glad when I became a stretcher bearer, 'So glad you'll be saving life, darling, instead of taking it,' she said. And I, though I think I would soon dump a stretcher and snatch a rifle if we were attacked, would I think, be haunted all my life if I knew I had killed anybody. I see the enemy too often as dupes rather than Fascists. I need to see a few atrocities, I suppose, and then I'd be a hard and merciless killer.

What an awful, depressing letter this is. I should write gay *triviata* but honestly, I can't. I think sometimes I ought not to write at all rather than like this. Sorry about the gloom of this letter, ducky, the mood will pass. Good night.

4.4.'44

Lovely Spouse,

Robert Lynd could write and perhaps is writing a charming essay about today for it is 4.4.44. The numerological incidence of which occurs once every eleven years. An idle fellow, Robert Lynd, I should think, an Izaak Walton who lives in the dappled shade of a willow tree, his back to the bole. If he's fishing there's no worm on the hook, for the rod is merely an excuse to sit there, idling by the pool. But this unusual cluster of fours from today's date would set him idly musing, and he would pitch the idea into the pool as he might a pebble and chronicle the rings as they widen. Idly, of course. A lovely life. I fancy it myself. So remote from the sheer sides of the 'soft underbelly' among the osiers, the frogs, and the leisurely flap of herons. Where? At Crowland, Wisbech or

87

Ely along the soft Nen or the peaceful Welland. The Nen, the Welland, the Great Ouse. I learnt these rivers at school, easily, remembering them, while the names of others passed out of my other ear, because of the lovely musical flow of their names. At school there were too few things like that, and among dates so few aids to memory, that apart from the Battle of Hastings I have retained none. That's why, if only in deference to future school children, I think we ought to finish the war this year, for 1944 is as easy to remember as 1066—how proudly the kids could trip it off. I guess we don't consider the children half as much as we ought.

'What do I think of the new General Forces Programme?' For that, I should take you sternly to task, for it is a crack of the worst type. There are radios in the army and there's a Field-Marshal's baton in every private's knapsack! On the rare occasions we've had a recreational wireless I've never been able to get near it. And when I've got within sight of it, it is only to watch some jive-fiend wriggling the needle in search of lumps of ether that are 'going to town'. That stuff is difficult to hear on account of the general hubbub going on. The quietest time is news time when, in the gaps between the infernal din of blokes shouting 'Quiet!' you may some-times, if you have an acute ear, detect Stewart Hibberd reading it. But for some time now we've had no radio, so can't even try to listen. I might reply by asking you what you think of the five-shilling Black Magic chocolates.

Andrew and I got a lift on the truck which was taking blokes to be deloused the other day, and although this involved us at the other end in a bit of a scene with the sergeant, who considered that we ought to go through the delousing process too, it enabled us to make an inspection of the little town which has been so frequently in the news. It was full of drawable bits. Over-rich with them so that you don't know where to start, but I was more interested in seeing the place. In the main square was the usual American sitting on the bonnet of the usual jeep, and there was the Amgot place with the townspeople jangling in the passage, there were girls with pots on their heads, a news sheet eight days old stuck on a wall, telling of the advance of the Red Army, and lots of little blokes with military hats and cloaks as unimpressive and as numerous as South American generals. There was a woe-begone woman of middle age, shabbily clad in black, who sat on the corner with her basket of washing and gazed miserably at nothing for an hour, and was still gazing when we left. And there was rubble, rubble blocking the steep cobbled side-streets, alleys might be a better word. And all around were knots of people with either nothing to do or no place to do it in. In the steep Giovanni Battista Strade some men were clearing debris and here we spoke to an old Italian who had lived in London, working on mosaic paving, and knew Leith and Edinburgh and therefore unreasonably perhaps made me feel a little nearer to Hawick. He complained of the French Colonial troops who were living in the town, with their wives! They were dirty, pulled down doors as well as fruit trees for their firewood. They are indeed poor propaganda for us, these troops, and though we are against any racial discrimination, putting them there seemed as erroneous as putting an Eskimo in a tube train and expecting him to know how to behave.

A few years of education in living is required before we can do this without offence as surely as it was before we became a nation of tooth-cleaners and nail-brushers. There were several shrines in the streets. We saw a woman making a fire in a frying-pan. She smiled. Maybe because she had something to cook.

The only work we saw going on, apart from hairdressing, was repair work. Carpenters and bootmenders sawing and banging away in dingy workshops with two-part stable doors. Few people seem to have any purpose, the French A.T.S. girls waddling briskly through the square contrasting noticeably with the lackadaisical, hopeless, do-nothing air of the natives. The coming and going of the armies, first German and then the numerous Allied; the imbroglio of the political situation is altogether too much for them. There was plenty of washing about, and we saw many shirts hanging on poles across the street from one balcony to another. The poles thrust through the sleeves of the shirts gave an unconscious symbolism, the appearance of a crucified man.

In one of the rooms of the Amgot building we studied a painted ceiling. Badly done and bought by the yard apparently and papered on, for there were dog ears hanging down. It was to these that Andrew said the figures were pointing in their pre-Fascist and classic plumpness. But to me they seemed to be passing the buck. 'He or she it was that was responsible for Fascism and the state of the country.' He or she and so on right round the room, all denying any complicity, like everyone does whom we meet here.

16.4.'44

Dear Spouse,

You have to remember numbers and there are so many of them in the army. A.L.63 is the number you want if you itch a lot. That is lice-powder. But I'm bad at figures. I thought it was A.B.64, which is pay books. Sprinkling yourself with those never killed any lice. Luckily, however, I found I wasn't lousy after all. Or perhaps they bit and departed, spitting me out. Once was enough. But why in this vein when I meant to be a bear? A bear? Yes, a bear and justifiably so. I've had no letters—well one—one in a fortnight. Which is not good enough. What's the big idea! Everybody else is getting thousands. Hicky nine in one day. Nine! Me—none. There are bottlenecks. Everybody moans over bottlenecks. umph! My bottleneck's got a cork in it! So I moan. G-r-r-r! But that's enough. I can't be a bear for long.

I have not been able to write to you for a week or so. But I have a good excuse. The blue-eyed Aryan again. It wasn't wise to write the way we were situated. We are again resting, now in beautiful surroundings where spring is positively singing and it's flat! So gloriously flat! And there are buttercups and primroses and birds and exciting buds everywhere and sprays of blossom. And I must not forget the stream. Clear, bubbling. So happy. Tall poplars, young, unclad as yet but dressing, primping themselves out in that wonderful green of new leaves—the most heartening colour in the world. Their trunks are long, slender, leggy and silver. So silver. So leggy. Lovely trees. And there's lots of insects for whom I have an affection—so long as they don't swarm. There are plodding beetles with six Charlie Chaplin feet and quivering antennae. And I never saw such a place for lizards. They rustle in the reeds (there's a yellow iris there) and last year's leaves and dart all over the place. There's bugloss and bird's-eye. Cattle white and slant-eyed, and women working in the fields, and way over the blue mountains growing young again as the warmth of the sun diminishes the white of their heads. And there's one little girl. I am quite captivated by her grace and her sad, quiet beauty. She has a dress of tattered blue, her hair is fair and braided, which gives her a dignity I have seldom seen anywhere. She has a quiet, wise look. You'd love her. Tomorrow, with her two little black-eyed charges, she is coming back for chocolate.

It's arrived. I knew it! The loveliest letter you've ever written, and it's over a fortnight old. I'll write a special letter tomorrow. Me and the nightingale who loves you too, who's telling the world so at this moment outside. He told it also in the front line, and told it so beautifully that I had to pause to listen when I should have been on my way to cover. Yes, we'll write a special letter tomorrow, and we'll dip our pens in moonlight. Good night. R.

8.5.'44

Dear Margaret Gunn,

The other day I was interviewed by a *Daily Express* war correspondent. We were back from the line again and I had some historic drawings about which Major Brock had told him, also I played a small part (very small) in the most exciting thing in this particular spot of action. Also—and he was particularly interested in this—I conducted the 'nearest to Jerry' wall newspaper ever. Actually on the wallpaper of a shattered house which we were holding—a wall which Bunny, an S.B. who came up with the relief, told me has since been knocked flat. He asked what I did with the drawings, and when I said I sent them to you, he didn't pursue the subject. I'm wondering now if he wanted them. I told him of our little incident—not much as you shall hear—but a thing which bucked the boys no end. Though when I get another spell of unbalanced thinking I shall regret what's coming in the shape of a black-bordered envelope to a certain German Fraulein. It's difficult for me to conquer this feeling.

The house was 150 yards from Jerry. We were to occupy and hold it without betraying our presence. To get us in, a thousand smoke shells screamed over, and the smoke was probed ever and anon by machine-gun fire. By night most of the boys were on guard most of the time; those that weren't, and slept, were shaken rudely should they begin to snore! As near as that! By night nearer, for Jerry usually sends out listening patrols. A general stand-to was called one night because, according to the sentry, one member of a German patrol actually came and stood in our doorway. The sentry, in the blackness of the interior, just watched him and let him go! The Jerry waved on five others and disappeared. Another sentry saw this, and why they held their fire I can only put down to sheer petrification from fright or an unusual devotion to orders! Anyway, the boys were alert for most of the night, with fingers on triggers or gripping grenades, and peering through each window and hole in the wall. I assisted on the wireless and 'phone. By night, like that, you see. By day, the artillery's war, we doing O.P. work for them and merely standing the shelling from Jerry. The O.P.—the main one (there were two below) was upstairs. To reach there, you climbed a ladder and crawled through a jagged shell hole in the floor. From here we could see the Swastika flags on the trees—on Hitler's birthday dozens of them appeared, and after an artillery stonk (lovely word) their stretcher bearers would appear, waving a tremendous Red Cross flag, and proceed slowly along with their casualties. So many appeared that we doubted the legitimacy of the cases and I drew a picture on the wall of 'Our neighbours conducting reliefs', which was interpreting the suspicion held by everybody that Jerry would carry his relief for any guard down by stretcher. All the same, they went unmolested. But just before dark Jerry would appear in considerable numbers to take up stand-to positions. They would scoot along the road as fast as possible.

Well, from our O.P. we had ranged artillery on the house into which we knew Jerry went. This we did in the afternoon, directing our shells till they were right on—'phoning back '50 yards west', '25 yards north' and so on. And our gunners were in readiness for the great stonk we requested at nightfall. That meant that about six different 'phones were held to six different ears, in relays, right back to the artillery, who were on their toes, lanyards in hand. We felt the whole army was behind us, that we were granted a terrible power. Our 'phone was in the cellar and we had to relay the message from the chap on O.P. duty through various rooms to it. I was one of the chain and that's all my part was. But two Jerries appeared. 'Oh—let them go!' A terrible power. Then about twenty, running. 'Sprint'—the code word—passed down from the O.P., all in whispers, for remember our nearness. 'Sprint' went along the chain to the 'phone, and 'Sprint' flashed along the various relays, right back to the artillery. They 'phoned back: 'They're on their way,' and immediately there was a deadly rushing whine and a whack! Jerry had had it. Direct hits. Terrible but necessary to win the war.

10.5.'44

My six days' rest camp was very short lived. It was a long

94

and very tiring journey in a bumbling truck over rotten roads
to get there—250 miles. The roads were white and dusty, the
trees alongside were also white and dusty as though they too
had come a long way and were resting from very exhaustion.
We missed meals to get there, eating only sandwiches. We
had been there only a day when we were recalled. All the
stretcher bearers. Tonight we were to go up to a symphony
concert, Mozart, Chopin and Rimsky-Korsakov! But we
started back.

One of the scandals here is the complete lack of any sort of
medical treatment for the Italians. Consequently, whenever
we pull out of the line, we are besieged by ailing Italians. So
it was last week. We had, for a few days, the best billets we've
had since leaving Hawick. In a farm, we slept on stretchers
in an outhouse. Every day we treated Italians who were
tortured with scabies. One was a little *bambino* of eight months
whose feet we bandaged every day. One chap, about 17,
came rushing in with an agonizing toothache. He was crying.
Toothache can be about the worst pain possible. And that he
has got to endure for lack of a dentist. We eased it temporarily
but could do nothing beyond that. One woman was in the
family way. We wondered about her and were relieved when
we left before she had it.

22.5.'44

I've had some lovely letters from you lately but all say that
your letters from me seem to be rationed to one a week. At
times that is unavoidable. These last two weeks particularly,
as you may have guessed from your newspaper. But some are
held for security reasons, whole shiploads of mail probably,

95

in view of what has been impending. I write at least once every two days when out of the line; when in it, well it's not possible. This letter is bound to be chaotic, which is not surprising, as I am chaotic. We all are at this moment. The papers are no doubt crowing about us and our achievements, but we aren't. We're bitter, for we've had a hell of a time, and are still pressing on. Everybody is out on their feet and one bundle of nerves. I can't tell you much yet and perhaps have already told you more than I should, but I can reassure you that the worst is over, and having come through the last nine days, will get through anything. But Chopper has been wounded, Stan and Ken Collins. Chopper a neat shoulder wound, Stan and Ken more serious, I believe, but with a good chance of pulling through. Percy was hit on the hand by shrapnel, fortunately only lightly. I was just alongside him. We've been Stuka'd, Mortared, Shelled, Machine-gunned, Sniped, and although we've taken Cassino, the monastery—that is our Div. and a few others—none of us feel any elation. We've cracked the hardest nut of the campaign but the losses sadden and frighten us. Attacking with the tanks, bullets everywhere, front, behind, the flanks—phew! At such times you can be ice cool, all the same you don't think much of your chances.

Pinned down behind a wrecked house with Steve, Percy, Tom, Buff and a few others, I made three sketches, and went so far as to put your name and address on them. I thought they would be my last. Unfortunately I lost them, though there is a slender chance they may turn up, since I left them in my Red Cross bag—which may reappear.

We got through that attack, and by next morning had cut the famous Route 6 which runs through to Rome. But, Girl, I'm glad you couldn't be a Polly Oliver after all for at times we've been near to insanity. Not at first, but after six days without sleep and without eating—we were all, and still are, very near to snapping. We've attacked, attacked, attacked from the beginning with numbers dwindling all the time. At the moment we are squatting in the cutting of the famous Cassino railway, expecting to be pushed into another attack. We had a hideous 'Stukaing' one day during a tremendous counter-attack. We sat in holes and trembled. Hicky cracked the day before, now Gordon did. A fairly new bloke, and cool normally, he had been wounded in the hand; and although he carried on, the shock of it didn't do him much good. He came scrambling out of his own trench to the one in which Steve and I trembled. To sit under a concentrated morning-long bombardment is—what? Hell is understatement. It's definitely unpleasant anyway. And poor Gordon scrambled in head first, crying: 'I can't stand it. I can't stand it—my head, my head.' And he clutched his head and wept. I wiped his forehead, neck and ears with a wet handkerchief, and sang to him. Next day he conquered himself sufficiently to come out with me wandering around sometimes in no-man's-land searching for casualties among burning tanks and ditches full of German dead. When, when, when is this insanity going to stop?

Just after writing that I was caught in some mortaring. He had this railway weighed up. I was lying flat, and 'clonk', a sickening lump of shrapnel landed close to my head. There are lots of fellows with packs riddled with bullets and cigarette cases pierced, for everybody has missed death narrowly so many times. Percy and I were in a house when it received four direct hits. Stuff came thumping down and half covered us. Then with the house rocking drunkenly we scrambled through the choking yellow dust and out. Later Buffin was hit. Arm again. So glad only his arm. Now, thank heaven, we're out of it for a time. Don't expect normal letters from me because I won't be normal for some time. But the positive thing is that we've done the hardest job, we've beaten him, we've driven him back. I wish I could concentrate on that and not be overwhelmed by the negative side of it all. Wish I were home with you, my darling.

Love,

ROBBIE.

24.5.'44

Lovely Wife,

'We are all together now, and behold one another's faces with comfort,' (Admiral Blake, writing home from the siege of Cadiz). The turbulence of mind is settling down and may be quiescent when the Rest Camp starts working its mollifying influence. I'm on the truck now, visiting the place again. Last time I was recalled after a day and thrown forthwith over the Rapido and there spent all my leave in battles more violent even than Peter's Corner! In battle with a leave pass in my pocket! They call it morale. During this period also I remembered it was my sister's birthday. I hope she spent a more pleasant day than I did. Chopper, Buff, Neville, Hicky, Childs and Taylor of the S.B.s are in hospital. Percy and Gordon Large were hit by shrapnel but carried on and Vernon Barker had a lump go through his water bottle. The stuff missed me like I was a leper. I hope it continues to do so. But it succeeded in shaking me considerably. There are so many stories I could tell you, so many horrors, but I shall try to push them all behind me for I do not wish to remember them or even retain them in my mind. That is true of all of us. A film show came to the camp. Is it a war film? Everyone asked. Had it been there would have been no audience. We should whoop over the positive side of things. We have broken his Gustav line and penetrated the Hitler line. But we are overwhelmed by the negative, the wild excesses of a vast, wild, powerful insanity.

I have reached the rest camp and am here for four days. Both cinemas are full and we are too late for a symphony concert. Am now in the club room.

Prior to going into action the last time I spent the better part of a morning sitting by a stream watching some women doing washing for the troops. One would have delighted the heart of any sculptor. I tried to draw her many times but couldn't capture it. A rough, wind-tanned peasant type, she had firm round limbs, jutting sculptored breasts, round arms, a rough grace and a tremendous amount of tireless peasant energy. These women have a marvellous way with dirty clothes. They stand barefooted in the running stream and using but little soap, they whack the dirty garments on the water one or twice, then knead the clothes towards them on the rock until they are a neat compressed pile beneath their strong hands. This is repeated several times with great energy and before long the greasiest and blackest garment is as white as any I've seen anywhere. Everybody remarks on this to me, who, putting a handkerchief through several boilings of Lux, Persil, Glitto and Vim, subjecting it to a soapy rubbing till I'm tottering on the brink of prostration, succeed in getting it to a colour which at best I can only term light black. The whole thing so primitively done seems nothing less than miraculous. I'll show you how they do it when I come home.

28.5.'44

I shall just write. Nothing so complete and rounded as a letter. The desire to achieve a complete letter results in many not being sent. Not so much in my case because I'm not so fastidious. I leave pencil lines in drawings and get nagged for it. It is the naggers who must fill a letter to the final cork. I shall probably just trail off. Interruptions will probably necessitate that, anyway. My letters might be divided into two parts. The discussion, the opinions, the theories, and the reporting. I have much reporting to catch up on before it slips my memory. For instance, about Cassino before the flare-up, when we, having taken over from the Guards, 'whispered about the place for a fortnight'. (Sinister pools in wide shell holes, silent, with the still stars deep down in them, reflection of a broken tank. Moon, smoke—and the smell of the dead.) And I have much to tell of the flare-up, and since. Of civil Italy. (At every meal kids waiting appealing with cans in which to collect what you don't eat, 30, 40, 50 kids, aye and wrinkled women. And there's porridge, bread and jam, and bacon bits, all mixed in some tins.) Tell you what I'll do. I'll give you some notes on Cassino, now, from my notebook.

A cellar at Cassino, 10 ft. by 14, 4 ft. high. You come in V-shaped after feeling your way through the hole in the floor above. Back brushes the concrete roof. Candlelight and shadows. (Light screened severely by night.) 'Where's Thomas and Jones, their turn on', and Gibby has to peer closely for them. And whisper: 'Thomas, Jones, where are you?' Both in this cellar. That's what the light's like. Snores. Heavy breathing. Sleepers. About seven of them. The hole through which you drop into here is a shell hole—jagged in the tiled floor above. You reach one leg down till you touch a crate of china. The former inhabitants here left it, I guess. With boards across it, it now forms our step. You clamber down and beware the two wire beds. Jerry put those there. Have cursed them in the night. Cursing beds—us who dream of them, who haven't slept in one for a year! Why—because we're so near the enemy. You wake up a bloke because he snores. 'Lay on your side!' At night the danger is nearer. Listening patrols may have crept forward. But this cellar. Three curtains (blankets) shield the feeble light. There are two concrete pillars eight inches square, two iron beams traverse the concrete roof. Blankets and mattresses on both sides of floor space. Floor, dark, earthy, smells mouldy. Who's here? Lt. Huckle, Sgt. Gibson, L/Cpl. Burnham, others in anonymity of shadow. Myself as S.B., L/Cpl. Ranger doing Signaller (38 set). Lies on his back slipping now and then into sleep but being jerked back every time like a boat on a painter. The buzz of the 'phone is mainly responsible, it also lies on its back by his ear. Ranger is a solicitor's clerk in Civvy Street. Young, a nice bloke, has impetigo on his chin. My most faithful patient, but conditions are all against improvement, can't wash, the water's rationed and there's swill from meals dumped in the rubble upstairs. Hellava lot of rubble, hellava lot of swill. The latrine is an oil drum and has to be emptied into a hole in another wreck of a room. Flies. The first mosquitoes. Fleas. And under the fallen rubble of the ruined staircase lies the body of a New Zealander. In the house. The pile has been shaped into some semblance of a grave. The German spade they did it with still lies there, substitute for a footstone. The twisted wrought iron of the staircase still hangs precariously over the grave. Another near bomb and it will come down, burying the Anzac still more. A rough wooden cross rests against the wall above the grave, neighbour to a stack of bricks and a box of assorted grenades. The cross says, baldly, '*Patterson. 2.N.Z.E.F.*' with '*R.I.P.*' pencilled down the spine. We cook by the grave and there's tea leaves on it and empty tins. Curious flowers indeed. But none of it is very sanitary and as the days wear on so the smells grow worse. Hicky has to venture from his house at night to sprinkle Lysol on bodies, it is impossible to bury them. Furniture is crammed against windows, splinters supporting splinters and reinforced by sandbags, bricks and rubble. There are religious pictures in various rooms skew-wise. Madonnas with uplifted eyes to heaven where the bombs come from. The room above the hole which is the entrance to the cellar is hexagonally tiled and strewn with plaster, matchsticks, kit, haversacks and ammunition. Flies dog-fight about the brass chandelier, or what is left of it. A door and a table-top lean in the tall window where once a woman cleaned the glass. There are two holes in the wall. First a small one. Keeping peers through this on to the Jerry position in the Hotel des Roses. The wreck of the Hotel des Roses you'll understand. Everything is wrecked here. Hole number two leads into the next room, we pass through it quite easily. The square above it says 'Keep out. Cookhouse'. A wicker chair is by the window. A sentry sits here at the Bren. It points at Castle Hill.

Tables and a low splintered marble-topped piece. On it? The usual assortment, ammo clips, cigarette tins, matches, bandoliers, boots wrapped in sacking, a tin of anti-malaria tablets and a hammer. The doorway is covered by a blanket.

Jerry can see through the broken wall beyond. A former occupant, Grenadier Guard, has been busy on the walls, where there are not grey scars left by falling plaster on the pink wallpaper hanging in tatters. He has drawn various women. Always women. The emblem of the Grenadier Guards is drawn too, and 3rd Battalion pencilled above it. And signatures of Anzacs.

2.6.'44

I had never seen a firefly until the night we crossed the Rapido. Then I saw thousands of them and most surprising things they are. Harry Routledge, Don R-ing, told me he pulled up several times in the belief that someone was waving a dimmed torch in the road before him. That is just about the candlepower—shall we say—of them and they go in and out during flight, which is a slow, wafting sort of affair. They twinkle right across the fields and look like the flashing of a distant artillery barrage. On either hand their myriad twinklings danced the scented fields, the moon shone large and the nightingale poured his heart out into the warmth of the night. In such an atmosphere we went into battle. Anne, in a lovely letter, tells how she used to wander along the Arno at Florence, hand-in-hand with a German, and remarks how unthinkable it must be to be fighting amid such loveliness. Anne remembered the fireflies, the loveliness also. It is indeed almost unbelievably lovely. I have yet to see a place that could be called ugly, in fact I have yet to see a spot that is not beautiful. At the moment we are in a tiny village, very small indeed but here I could draw for a month and still not exhaust subjects. It abounds with animal life, hens, pigs, goats, sheep and cattle, and this morning I was climbing the steep street, when a goat popped its head out of the door to see who was making such a clatter on the cobbles. Being in a whimsey mood I said good morning to it, and I don't think I should have been surprised if it had asked me in. The front doors are nothing like our front doors and you are totally wrong if you visualize a bright green door with a knocker. You even might have imagined a garden with a privet hedge. They are mainly rough wooden doors, often of the stable-door type with a swing top. And they lock from inside with a wooden bar, or having locks demand a key of gaoler proportions. These Mussolini probably called in with the wedding rings, as each one has enough iron for a couple of tanks and an armoured car at least.

8.6.'44

The news! Yes, the news! The Invasion is a fact! A fact! Rome was the button. I see the West Kents have recognition, in the press, of being the boys to make the break through from which all this followed. Tut-tut! You may kiss me though. The counter will be held, and perhaps it may be home for Christmas and Hawick for Hogmanay. Terrific upsurge was apparent here. Last night we had a set of earphones, each end in a mug for amplification and a dozen chaps pressed round it to listen to the King's speech. Yesterday a truckload of Italians went by singing, and a board on the roadside displayed in chalk the triumphant note '2nd Front has started, official'. When the radio set is working it has a crowded audience. But we're busy here now and seldom get the chance to listen to it. This letter is being written on a truck in convoy

—during the stops. The roads are bumpy, my bottom likewise and painfully tender. Don R's pass us looking like mil-
lers—jeeps go by and lumbering trucks—the jerky, lumbering,
stinking, all-important supply line to keep Jerry reeling. It's
every member a living palimpsest of dust, veneer laid upon
veneer. They look like white niggers dusted instead of black
about the eyes, a cracked grease-paint appearance. I shall be like
it myself when we've been under way a bit longer. The dust is
on this paper, the pen is ploughing. Italian civilians are trickling back with bundles, bikes and *bambinos*. Some will find
their villages miraculously intact, others terribly battered—
the penalty for choosing to live in defensible areas. Bailey
bridges are over the gaps left by blown ones, in a trice.
You've got to hand it to the Sappers. But some Jerry has had
no time to blow up.

But what an intensely rich 'plain' this is. It still undulates
and really hasn't a great deal of plain-ness about it, getting the
title only by comparison with the many mountains, but
everything is lush and rich on it. The peasants are sweeping
with their scythes among tall grass, the corn is shining a
deeper gold every day and the ears are fat and firm. Olive
trees abound and farm folk move among them spraying them
with pipes attached to a canister worn pack-wise on their
backs. Grape vines climb horizontally between the olives and
the hot sun dazzles on the waxy fountains of the maize plants.
These remind me strongly of aspidistras. The poppies are
holding mass meetings in the fields and the subject must be
the Second Front, for nothing else could make their red bon-
nets nod so eagerly. There are hosts of wild flowers of all
sorts, no wonder the birds sing as they do. And the breeze is
among all that, swaying the grass. And when you look a long

time wondering what the 'something different' is about all
this verdure, it suddenly dawns on you. It is the way it
crowds. All the crops seem to be jostling as furiously and
densely as women at the start of the village-hall jumble sale.
And none seem the weaker for the struggle but stronger for
it, and so thrust up, green, fat and crowding. We must certainly come here in peacetime.

Pierre, the sixty-year-old member of the Intelligence Section, an apple-cheeked Italian who drinks, and having drunk,
weeps for the 'Poor boys who didn't come back last time', is
largely responsible for picking billets when we are near villages. Billets for the Padre, the M.O. and the Officers' Mess.
For nearly always we sleep in our pup tents. But we decided
we had found the ideal billet and we said we would get Pierre
to reserve it for us. But it was far, far away from where we
usually are. It was roomy, though, and I think you would
approve and indeed clamour to share it, even though it
would mean a four-flight descent to collect the morning milk.
It was the Piccini Theatre, Bari. I shared a box in the theatre
with Andrew and Bob Patten, seeing my very first symphony concert. The orchestra was sixty strong and conducted
by a young chap. They began with the Air on a G String,
followed by two arias from the 'Marriage of Figaro' sung
beautifully by a comely soprano. They also gave us Mozart's
40th, absolutely one of my favourites. They finished with a
terrific piece called, I think, 'The Polovtsian Dances'. That
was my first concert, and was just fine. It took four excitable
Italians, swarthy, dark, and all of the same diminutive size, to
show us to our box, also a grey-haired old lady with a broom
and a boy. We were somebody! We gave the boy a lordly
10 lire. We just had to, after all that. But I felt that there were

stories about these people and the theatre, the thick-maned little men with their blue chins and blue serge suits, the wrinkled old lady, and the boy. The theatre itself, besides its stairs, had long low vaulted corridors, and a bar with a boarded-up door. The feeling of a story was strong in that too, a story bound up with these people. I thought for some reason of Quilp and the Old Curiosity Shop, though the resemblance might be puzzling to find. The audience had many Poles among it. What strongly national faces they have! And the royal box was occupied by men in hospital blue.

12.6.'44

My Lady Gunn,

The town before me sat on the hill like a dunce's cap, and as I drew it from the shade of an olive grove in which we were resting, I pictured you coming down the steep streets on a donkey in the manner of the Italian women, and carrying as they often do a keg of wine each side of the saddle. The town goes higgledy-piggledy down the hill, and if it was planned at all, it was planned over very strong vino with the night well advanced. But I have a strong fancy, which I'm sure you will share with me, to live in such a place after the war. It isn't that I would like travel, I wouldn't any more—not at least how the tourist understands it, but there are quite a few places I would like to live in for a while, and that seems to me to be the only way we might satisfy the wanderlust and the desire for a family. I imagine there will be a strong partisan feeling among our children. The first, born a Scot perhaps, will be hot in argument about the merits of Scotland as opposed to the second's claims regarding Italy. No fear of a parochial outlook among our bairns and *bambinis*.

We could advance to within a very short distance of this town by transport, and on the way a Don-R pulled alongside to ask us if we would take three civilians aboard. They were English, he said. But they weren't, they were South Africans. Escaped prisoners! They had been taken at Tobruk and had been at large ever since the invasion of Italy. They looked bronzed and brown and very happy. But they hadn't been well fed, though they had nothing but praise for the Italian folk who had fed them from their meagre supply. With these they had worked as farm labourers most of the time, living in caves and often in the village, and moving among the Germans all unsuspected. They feared the Fascist Italians naturally, and it is a good assessment of popular feeling among the peasants that they weren't startled once. They still wore army clothes, but dyed. They told us that 4,000 had escaped with them, and that many were still at large, but many had given themselves up because of hunger. It must have been exceptionally trying during the winter. They looked blank when we told them the Second Front had started, they didn't know the expression!

It is good going through these smaller towns and villages. In this one people cheered and crowded to watch us go through, and on the trees were such greetings as 'You are welcome', 'Kill all Germans', and 'All Germans are gangsters'. And a grizzled old boy in blue jeans was dishing out drinks as fast as his one glass and narrow-necked bottle would permit him to. We were told that the Germans had shot 25 of the local people.

I have yet to see a Jerry who has been fighting without

heavy dress. And in most cases with full equipment. Nearly always, both in North Africa and here, we have gone in in shirt-sleeved order. O.K., by day, but at night when you're dug in and are squatting and dozing in your little foxhole you more than wish for your jacket. Those nights there is no chance for blankets to come up—and one night during the Rapido breakthrough it rained. The dawn is very welcome then.

15.6.'44

In Italy it is Uncle Bill, not Uncle Joe. You would think that anyway, for they write W. Stalin on the walls. It means *Viva* and is really two overlapping v's. We met a communist, he told us of the castor-oil methods of Fascism during his twenty years' enforced silence. He asked about Senor Oswaldo Moseley! He was bald headed, stout and gave a beautiful impression of Mussolini over a glass of vermouth. He was in fact similar in build to Musso, though somewhat larger and his impression was not the usual one of a ranting Benito, but of the flaccid lesser-known kind. Hand on hip and bouncing on his toes. Quite good.

Bari divides itself into three distinct cities, the old city, squalid, strangely built, all slum and churches—'What jerwant, Joe,' the kids asked when we went there, and then there's the industrial city down by the railway, and, lastly, quite a Bournemouth-looking part. White buildings, prom-enades. It is of course on the Adriatic. But the largest, noblest(!) buildings of all were the barracks and the jail. Terrific. And yet there are holes in the opposite pavement which one could easily fall into and incur serious injury. There was a wonderful promenade of people and outlandish costumes. The Italian army certainly went in for these in a big way. Yet there is nothing scruffier than an Italian in an old uniform. Alongside 'em your husband is a glittering sartorial jewel. Sunday evening a motley crowd gathered at the water's edge. We nosed. Two barefooted longshoremen, boats nearby, were selling octopuses. Small and white, but octopuses all the same, and therefore objectionable. Not so to the natives. They were eating them raw! Giving a tentacle to a child in a pram, handing a couple to the wife and four to the husband. In short a grand stand-up alfresco family meal—and all in their Sunday best, too. It is surprising how many good suits and frocks have survived the war. The octopuses cost 10 lire each, but even Andrew, who'll have a go at most things, quailed at this. We bought one for a little girl and she enjoyed it hugely, smiling at us over a mouthful of tentacles.

Joe Rose and Bob Langridge formed a two-man deputation to me the other evening. 'We've decided', said Joe in his usual stentorian boom, 'that we don't want your old woman living in our district.' All the same he gave me the address of his mother. I think he'd like you to call on her, I guess it'll make his ma feel a little nearer her Joe. He has one brother, a prisoner in Germany, while another, young John, was killed with us in Africa. Joe was a coalman so there's a chance you'll come away carrying a half-ton of coal.

Phew! It's awfully close and airless in here. I can't think, and the pushing of this pen causes the sweat to flow. Good job we aren't fighting in it at the moment. It would be lovely to sit at a café table with my wife, though.

Been very busy these last few days providing entertainment and bringing in money for the Casualty Fund at the same time. Entertainment has been nil lately, and the boys billeted in the blazing sun or pouring rain alternatively with, for two days, no tents, not being allowed out, and being miles away from everywhere, were having a justifiable moan. However, the game provided good entertainment, like an enlarged parlour game. It was a race track, taped and pegged off into rungs about 40 yards long overall. I made six plywood horses (rather burlesqued steeds) and they are lined up. Two dice are thrown. First one denotes which horse moves, second how many rungs he moves. And we run a tote which keeps half a dozen clerks going like mad all the time. A race-card is made, and hurdles and handicaps included. It sometimes gets quite exciting, the betting is fast and the odds are good. How popular it is may be gauged from the fact that a 10 per cent cut on the tote has realized 30 pounds for the fund in two days! The money paid out must be near the 300-pound mark. We also made a Derby sweep which raised 40 pounds for the fund. These things mean quite a lot of work for me, and this letter is being rushed I'm afraid, because in twenty minutes I've got a fund committee meeting. Seven people, dependants, are going to get 20 pounds. Not bad going.

20.6.'44

We are completely immured, but it's lovely all the same. We're deep in a trough of rolling landscape, mainly golden. Swaths of corn lie about and many fields bristle like a cat's back with stalks. And the sturdy peasant girls are busy at work with sickles. No people are more important, and if we are apt to forget it in less troubled times, the lesson is emphasized in war. There are queer little ricks designed by Emmet, and they stick comically on the skyline. The ricks are round, and all through winter they slice them down, working round them and leaving a slender apple-core of a stick leaning drunkenly and supported by props. There are heavy white, long-horned cattle with calves, Eastern-looking cattle, oxen they might be, with mystical oblique eyes. There are pigs and a frisky young donkey who skips about his laden mother, making her journey lighter perhaps by his high-kicking friskiness, or more likely by his juvenile abandon, making her very conscious of her load. One day the youngster, too, will be a dejected beast of burden, but ducking his head now and flourishing his heels, racing on ahead and curvetting round his patient parent, he seems blissfully unconcerned by the prospect. He is very lovely. I'd like to buy him for you. The farmhouse had two yawning shell holes—Jerry was here not so very long ago, but went in too much of a hurry to take the cattle with him. There's a sensuous rhythm in the lines of this country which quite excites. When it stops raining I'll try to draw some of them, but today the clouds have been scowling across the sky and the rain has teemed down, drawing many of the fellows from their bivvies to the shelter of this very convenient cave in which I am at the moment. I feel very damp and rheumaticky. Jimmie Fevin shares my joy in this peasant countryside. He joined us recently. He is a pleasant youngster, cool, unperturbed and considers with me that the world is too helter-skelter. He has a countryman's wit, but it is a sleepy mumble in a pleasant deep voice. He dreams of dawdling hay-carts with himself nodding on top and the horse pulling up at the local and saying: 'Hey Jim, what about a half?' All the horses are like that in Jimmy's Somerset. They know all the stops and always call in the grocer's for sugar.

'Sometimes they go right in, they forget about the cart they're pulling.' When Jimmy goes home on leave the village copper says: 'Ah, young Jimmy's home, have to keep on eye on that young shaver.' But Jimmy gives the impression that, given a pig's back to scratch occasionally and a half o' cider of nights, he'd ask for nothing else. He has a mature countryman's philosophy. 'We ought to like one another and help one another like we do in Somerton, and enjoy the little things so many people did, like hearing the birds sing and watching the crops.' The battle of Sedgemoor was fought quite near Jimmy's village, and he has a droll way of comparing present war strategy with that. He sounds like he fought in it. He tells, too, the story of the vagabond husband who lurches home drunk at least once a week and wallops his wife. One day both were drunk and they harnessed up the horse, not noticing that they were putting the shafts through a five-barred gate. 'They climbs on to the wagon and spends all afternoon belabouring the horse in turns,' says Jimmy. He's a good laddie.

It's still raining, unbelievably hard. It's even coming through the roof of the cave now.

25.6.'44

Hullo—Tethered to a queue perhaps, how these odd moments begin to add up—Quoted from *The New Statesman* and appreciated more by you than me. How do you kill the time in those trying waits? I have always hated them and— I forgot it just now—in the army have probably had longer and more numerous waits than you have, after all. Every mealtime officially, though I mainly manage to avoid these by turning up late, every pay-parade, Naafi, inoculation. Without a book I refuse, if possible, to become part of these bovine processions. Discussion often prevents the opening of the book, but it is there to fall back on. Anyway, I'm glad you liked the letter I sent you written in a queue, and pleased that you have had three nice letters. I've sent you so many lately that I think I would be ashamed to read whining, self-pitying things of no possible cheer to you. They haven't been brave, firm, cheerily swashbuckling. Though recognizing the part we are playing, they show no desire to play it further. They have been personally defeatist, have they been cowardly?

We all know fear, and I think the best antidote to it is the steady carrying out of your job. It is strange, but it is not so much the fear of death with me, as a fear of never seeing you again, of never embarking on our wonderful plans. It is that that frightens me. But now it is more serious. Hicky after seeing many tough types taken out of the line, bomb-happy, tearful and shaking, said that he was surprised that those kind went when the more nervy, highly-strung blokes like us were able to carry on. Well, Hicky went last time; and I am, we all are, in the S.B.s, more nervy. The nerves get worn. Way out of the line, we react slightly to gunfire, though we know it's only practice stuff—and our own planes passing over provoke a nervousness we never felt before. It's only small perhaps, but it's there, and it may increase. Really I suppose we all need a period of convalescence, even perhaps with treatment. In the line again we'll be all right, but for how long? We won't manage for so long without sleep, we won't be able to stand the same amount of fatigue. If we try it, I'm afraid the nerves will win, and we'll go back psycho-neurotic cases. I wonder if we shall be problem men. There'll be a world full of them—civvies, children too—if the peace doesn't provide sufficient rehabilitation.

I've seen men duck at the buzzing of a bee, and a whole platoon go to ground when a chap innocently gargled his throat. And consider the case of the sentry who fell and accidentally shot himself when we were in static positions earlier on. He was an awkward carry down the mountain side, and before we got him to the R.A.P. he was murmuring in delirium: 'The Dodecanese, we've lost all those islands now.' He was saying: 'Where were the aircraft. Poor lads, they didn't stand a chance. Oh, Jerry, you wicked beggar—oh, they didn't stand a chance.' And so on. And though we were taking him in with a wounded leg he was complaining about his chest, that he couldn't breathe—because he was wounded there in the Dodecanese. Now the stuff on that man's mind! And how much are we going to be affected in the same way, and will it change us much?

I don't want to frighten you, darling, and it may be that I have overstated it, but something of what I said is there. We treat it with humour, this nervousness. Lil, for instance, must never say 'Shell the peas' to Hermy when he gets home. She must find another word for it. And he fears that when he is loath to dig the garden, she will make unscrupulous use of his condition and slam a few doors, whereupon he will immediately start to dig trenches with great fury. Maybe it is this humour that will save us. The war cannot last much longer, that is a comfort. Let us hope that no devilries of poison gas and fresh infernal weapons are exploited.

I want the cottage on the edge of the village about which you wrote in your lovely last letter, I want the walks home

under the elms when the leaves are whispering lullabies to
the young rooks, and on across the stream where the water
lilies are, and where, if we are very still, we may catch the blue
of a kingfisher. Don't the willows remind you of Isaak
Walton? And there, if we are quiet we may watch the vole
on the bank rubbing his little paws over his face in his
nightly ablutions. . . .

How high and how wide is the hurdle of time we both long
to jump?

27.6.'44

I have just read Fontemara, his peasants 'turn round and
say'. The English do that, I've always noticed it. 'He turned
round and said this, so I turned round and said so and so.'
This always conjures in my mind the rather absurd picture
of the English conversing and pirouetting like ballet dancers
as they do so. It would be a gay world if we did, so it would if,
on frosty mornings, instead of falling down one at a time, we
all fell down together.

I don't like the idea of the pilotless plane. The reports are
played down here, not exaggerated as you suggest they might
be. We had the impression that they came over singly about
once a day. When we read of the authorities interviewing
people in the street about them, we knew. Everybody seems
to have seen them. Keep your nut down, girl. I should say
it's not difficult to locate their drones, unless they turn in the
air. But what a diabolically new phase of war this opens.
There simply must not be any more wars, for with the development of these things the world will be able to shell itself
to bits without ever leaving its own doorstep. And here we've

found chemical warfare dumps. That means gas. And as he grows more desperate. . . . I much prefer my gay world. That's a harmless lunacy.

Know what today is? My fourth anniversary of joining up! And still a private. As a matter of fact I turned down promotion only today; not the first time. I dare say that exasperates you, but I'll tell you why someday.

20.7.'44

This won't be a very cheerful letter. Percy Ross was killed the other day. I've got his wallet here. It's got two shrapnel holes in it, and they've gone right through pictures of Percy as a boy in the school football team, Percy just starting work, and Percy as a soldier. Through pictures of his mother and Hilda, and through letters from Hilda. I've been trying to write to Hilda but can't, poor kid, I keep thinking about her. Percy didn't know much about it. There wasn't a sound. A cloud of dust, a choking smell and a ringing in my ears. I expected to see them scramble clear, but there was young Percy, and young Tony Konstantinou, the Cypriot, and two others lying still on one side, two more dead on the other, and Tom Meadows and myself standing untouched in the middle. There were wounded too, all from one shell. We got the wounded into a house. I joined up with Percy, know his family, knocked about with him all this time, nearly always sharing the same tent. Donkin, the jeep ambulance driver, told me not to take it too hard. He took the wounded back, got 'em off, returned to his jeep, and 'whack!' he got it too. He was another great guy. And Don, the Yank ambulance driver, went up on a mine. It was as bad as Cassino. And longer. One casualty they couldn't wake. Shake, pinch, slap him, he still slept on. So we sent him back out of it.

They were pleased way back because it was some advance, and the Brig. sent a Don-R up to tell us: 'Well done, West Kents. You're the most forward battalion in Italy.' But the most forward battalion didn't whoop, it was too desperate. And there'll be more vacant chairs at the reunion dinner we have so often talked about. It's a strange battalion these days. Far different from that at Hawick. Maxie wouldn't know many now. You can tell, for as far as action goes, there's only about half a dozen who have seen as much as I have, and for actual company work which brings you closer to the enemy, I'm almost alone. That's a pretty grim commentary.

There's a terrific irony about the deaths of Percy and Tony. Two days before, we had been getting in the wounded. Percy went back with Tony on a second journey to a house where they had several bandaged up. Getting in, they found Jerry in occupation, smoking and talking to the casualties, who included Germans also. Percy and Tony smoked with them, got on famously. 'They were smashing blokes,' they said. Two helped them back with the wounded. They passed Hermy and me, who were having a long job with a broken pelvis. Two Jerries, the London and the Cypriot boy, with the wounded on a stretcher, and the Red Cross flag. It was in the Jerries' power to take them both prisoners, they didn't and we know how it worked out. Wish they hadn't been such smashing blokes.

I hear that Percy is being recommended for the M.M. He did many brave things. The award is not for one specific thing, but for what is more difficult to maintain—a high standard of behaviour all the way through.

Let's try to be brighter now. Oh, dear! It's always that now. Let's try to be brighter. But we've got to do it for the same reason that we have concerts when we are out of the line, for the same reason that many blokes get drunk. It keeps the memories and the ghosts outside the door. It's a desperate sort of gaiety. When a chap is abstracted and broody over a drink you know why, and you know what he is thinking about. I went round to the R.A.P. last night. That's the Doc.'s headquarters and focal point of the stretcher bearers. Steve and Hermy were out and very forcibly I realized there was nothing, and how very barren everything was. Steve and Hermy are all that remains of the real old boys, the Hawick people, all that are left of the crowd that gave the stretcher bearers a name that is famous throughout the division.

I'm sorry about these letters. I'm sending mostly this sort lately. That's because the life we lead is full of it. You can play football when you are out of the line, go to pictures, concerts, and it's O.K. so long as you are running away from it, but when you sit down with a blank sheet of paper before you your thoughts come up, and though you don't want to write them they are strong enough to condemn any levity. They're like a conscience. It is necessary to develop into hard live-for-the-day fatalists. The fighting soldier must be that. Then he may exult at the advances of the army as a whole, and not brood over the losses that go with victory. But it seems to me that he gets nearer to the animal then. I shall write you tonight, something less depressing.

24.7.'44

Dear Wife,

'Crisis in Germany.' Thus blare the headlines of the *Union Jack* just a few hours after I was elevated to the ranks of non-commissioned officers. I see now that by refusing promotion for so long I have served only to prolong the war. The Japanese Cabinet is in a flap too, and though I consider it unseemly jubilation, and likely to turn a fellow's head, I have a feeling a salvo will be fired to honour my stripe from the surely white-hot guns of the Kremlin. I feel, too, that now I can live up to my civil servant wife. Actually I was cornered. 'I know you prefer to be a free-lance, but there's nothing else for it,' explained the Doc. So here I am, not having troubled to sew the stripe on yet, but causing repercussions in the Reich already.

I had an enjoyable evening last night. Bob took me to see some paintings done by an Italian friend of his. I fancy they were copies, but very capably done, considering the girl who did them was no more than eighteen. (That's sounds rottenly patronizing, the N.C.O. touch.) But Bob, Killer Gorman from Wigan, Vernon Baxter and about six or seven of the family—Grandfather, Grandmother and all sorts—sat about sipping some splendid wine and eating baked pears, boggling and laughing at the language problems and—singing in turn! I sang them 'Ole Man River' (ah *basso profundo*) and surprised them and myself with a rendering of something from *Tosca*. Then we all had another go in turn. Wish you could have been there, it was the best evening I've had for a long time.

We've had hectic entertainment laid on for us at this village.

It's high up, with a wide view over the green *campagna*. We've had pictures, shows, football, and even a dance in the square which was rather a fiasco. And we're billeted in a school, to the detriment of the equipment—and when and if the kids have a school now I don't know. The occupation of schools should be avoided wherever possible.

I have hundreds of coloured pencils now, the boys found a Fascist stationer's shop. Steve, who is now a sergeant, got Indian ink and books, all sorts for me. I would like you to count up all the drawings you have received from me, just idle curiosity, but idly insistent all the same. This is a rotten letter. How much longer is this going to last? I don't want to write, I want to talk to you, talk far into the night. However, I have early hopes, for Ernie Rice tells me that the Russians are advancing on 'Walsall'.

6.8.'44

Mio caro,

The Partisans hearten one. Three came through a *villagio*, wearing red scarves and German Smeisers at their hips. They passed out, advancing in file, and gave us the clenched fist salute of the Brigate Garibaldi. The walls were plastered with notices, 'The people of Florence welcome the liberating Allied armies, 'Viva Brigate Garibaldi'. A pamphlet was prominent among them. 'The dead, ours and yours, demand that we intensify the struggle against the common enemy.'

I'm very tired. It's been very long, and taken its usual toll, including poor Jackie Rudling.

We halted and were housed in this village. In a fine though modest house. Little Liliano gave us another leaflet, and ironing in a cubby hole was Renata. She quite took my breath away. *Molto bello!* I was absently singing 'Your tiny hand is frozen' and then Anita (wife) and Guido came in, followed by Renata. We had made a top-note entry. The four of us, S.B.s, had the happiest part of the house, with the family. I have three good boys with me, including the pleasantly rural Jimmy Fevin from Zummerzet, whom everybody takes to. The table was laid *subito* and beds prepared. Our concern that we might be turning them out was calmed by the assurance that they all slept down in the *rifugio* while the shells still came over. I wished that you could have been there. The Italian picks up apace when we are with civilians, but it is still very much of the pidgin variety and there is still too much *Io non capisco*, which is a sad admission for a would-be schoolmaster.

Liliana is delightful. She skips with Jimmy and makes spaghetti with a tiny bowl, a morsel of flour and a pencil for a rolling-pin. But she cheats at 'Fly away Peter, fly away Paul'. Renata was excited, her brother, who belongs to the Brigate Garibaldi, was coming here. But though she says she saw him, he didn't come to the house, so I didn't meet him. Anne's city of Florence reclines among the hills. It looks lovely. Certainly the country through which we have approached it is glorious, though ideal for defensive purposes. Looking back on it from local vantage points I marvel how we managed to overcome it. Our army is no mean force now. That I seldom enthuse over its deeds is because I, and we its vanguard, are hit so hard personally by it, and because I as a stretcher bearer see and deal with wounded and dead all the time, and they are all people I know and have soldiered with so long. I have seen so many go. Of the fellows who actually get to grips, only Chopper and I are left now, of our original platoon, and I am the only one who has got away absolutely scot free. Chopper, likewise Buff, is still away, though Stan is back with a not-quite-right shoulder, but a functionable one. The other day I said to Jacky Rudling: 'If we can stay alive for six weeks I reckon we'll be O.K.' But poor Jacky got a direct hit on his trench. Still, don't fear; we're resting at the moment, the six weeks will fly, and then . . .

10.8.'44

'Tis evening and *molto* hot, rendering moist the brow. I love you to distraction. *Mio caro fidenzate*, but instead of holding up the glad tidings to tell you, I should get cracking. The tidings are these: we are out of the line and all of one piece, a fact which surprises the quartermaster. 'You dodged them again?' he said. Which shows you that some people, among whom I include myself, consider I enjoy great luck. Thus I am one of the few originals left.

The boys are now exploring the town. I write in a Catholic classroom with black-gowned churchmen floating ever and anon past the door. Buff and Chopper are back and in their usual form. I was giving Italian lessons on the board this morning. Buff quietly tut-tutted. Charterhouse isn't what it was. He asks me to give the *bella signorita* his love, and if she hears melodious music beneath her window one night 'tis the Count returned, Count Bruno Buffin. He tells an amusing tale of the ambulance train chugging through the night, filled with wounded, many moaning, and the nurse walking up and down saying: 'My little niece collects German badges, has anybody got any German badges?'

Soon we shall be on leave. *Molto opera, si?* It will probably be Rome. We fought up to it and beyond, but got no more than a distant view of it. So with Florence. Hard fighting brought us to within two kilos of it, and it spread white and beautiful among the hills below us. And there, oddly enough, we had a really good time. We were no longer in the wilds of the hills, but in a village, where we slept in beds and were on extremely good terms with the people. I met a fine family there and Renata was the belle of the village. I was envied by all the boys when she walked down the village street with me. I used to take her along to see the Doc. when we wanted to replenish our medical supplies, and we would air our Italian, while Joe, the fat ambulance driver from Ohio, would butt in to ask what about a spot of lend and lease. The village was still under shell fire. Renata has a dashing partisan brother who managed to get into the village several times. We were treating him for advanced scabies—but under somewhat difficult circumstances, since he was always off to join his unit in no time. He was keen, his smile flashed, and for all his dashing red scarf, red star, brown legs and shorts, one couldn't help imagining him in doublet and hose with a rapier at his side—a cavalier of Tuscany.

The villagers all slept in a communal *rifugio*; we weren't turning them out of their beds. Domenica (Sunday) we had a tremendous feed of spaghetti. Lovely, and possibly to save us the embarrassment of twirling it on a fork, it was cooked, not in thin strings, but in a fatter and more manageable way. Anita was nice, she was the wife of Guido. Aldo, their son, was about thirteen, and Liliana, whose beauty has never been surpassed, was seven, full of mischief and a wrench to leave. Jimmy Fevin and Mitch were asleep one afternoon. I was

swotting Italian. Liliana came in, and hardly containing herself, prattled excitedly to me in Italian, taking me into a deep
plot. But I was a base-wallah in this plot, Liliana would carry
out all the action. The action? Tickling Jimmy's feet. Oh,
it was grand fun. We kissed them all when we left, including
Guido: an old Italian custom.

17.8.'44

Dearly Beloved,

I look out of our billet, which is quite a good house with
excellent ceilings chock-a-block with apple-bottomed cherubs.
With so many un-napkined *bambinos* above me I confess to a
strong apprehension lest one disgraces himself all over me. I
am wriggling at the roots. Not wriggling really, that's not the
word. What is it that responds to beauty? The feeling is nearly
a wriggle, of the pores, capillaries and cells perhaps, an exquisite
near-pain akin to wriggling the toes in the seaside mud. I get
that feeling when I look at those lovely roofs. Each roof is
composed of a collection of voluptuously carved tiles, and
each of these tiles has absorbed the sun for years. Mellow
roofs. And down below is a cobbled garden with a fig tree,
with wide green hands. An Italian granny sits on the steps in
the shade sorting oats—why I don't know. And gay on the
cobbles, singing and always busy, go Laura and Eleanor, English names of attractive twins who have a tremendous capacity
for work, washing and needleworking in the garden from
dawn to dusk. But the picture reminds me strongly of sets
from the old Ronald Coleman-Vilma Bankey films, she the
peasant girl, he the dashing Hussar. You may not remember,
child, too young. But they used to fascinate me. In a Hun-

garian setting or Ruritanian Prisoner of Zenda setting, here it is all over again and in real life.

At the moment Jenkins is down there, thoroughly at home though knowing not a word of the language. Come to this little town, lovely. There was a sun-drenched street the other day, narrow and shady too, peaceful and drowsy and from somewhere came the soporific sound of a slowly fingered piano. And there's a donkey, and a little boy filling a can at a pump in the middle of a square, and shutters are over the windows like sleepy lids, there are churches and bells and arches and a cemetery on the hillside set with cypresses. Even the ducks cease their quacking in the afternoon and settle down in a doorway, bills tucked away in comfortable wings. Sun. Sun. Sun. Dust. Grapes, melons, plums drying on roofs; groups of women at wells in the shade of a porch, persecuted by flies, a cripple girl in a bath chair. Below, the town, suddenly flat—flat as the fens, the wide *campagna* with dusty roads and weighting vines till it brings up sharp against the mountains.

20.8.'44

Why, if it isn't my dear own Margaret Gunn! I may well show surprise, since for four days we've been strangers, and I'm afraid it is my fault entirely. In action the chances to write are limited, and they are not plentiful immediately we come out of the line, either. This is mainly due to the Casualty Fund and the work it throws on my not too sturdy shoulders. This week, you see, we are sending, to ten lots of dependants, twenty pounds each. This involves not only the writing of letters on my part—and they are difficult—but the stimulating

of collections, the launching of various money-making enter-
prises, and all sorts of things. The latest being that I now do
portraits to raise money, having for that purpose a studio in
this lovely old town. It is a fund office, too, and I have a
beautiful long desk with pull-out drawers.

I really want a full-time stenographer, one who is a good
organizer. I am thinking of sending for you. I really need you,
for you would weep if you saw the muddle the closed drawers
conceal. I'm afraid I could never be tidy for more than a day.
I did start it well, too. But now all the stuff for the 'In' tray
finds its way into the ash tray, and the ash tray finds its way
into both the 'In' and the 'Out' tray. I could use you for a
model too, how would you like to be a forces' favourite
pin-up? I would feed you on melon and peaches and plums
which abound here, and occasionally an early grape.

I have twinges of regret about this portrait business, as I
see so many lovely bits of the town which I want to draw and
which now I may not find the time to do. Tomorrow, however, I shall be evicted. The eviction lasts for two days, and
comes about because in one tiny room in this fairly large
building they occasionally make acid. When they do that the
whole building has to be evacuated on account of the fumes.
That's fairly typical of Italy. One day some great man of
vision is going to point out that the acid could be made elsewhere and the business of the town can carry on uninter-
rupted. Maybe the evicted people get paid for the days out,
and like it as it is. I overlooked posters. I usually produce one
or two of these.

Another landing in France today. Jerry must feel like he's
living in a swing door and all parts hitting him. I don't think
you need worry a lot now, for with luck I need make no

more demands on my incredible good fortune. To think I
may never have to duck again!

22.8.'44

Fishing is out! And don't prattle with the bloke behind you
in the office if he puts ideas like that in your head. I have read
H. A. Manhood on salmon fishing in the Irish lakes. It is
always a great battle of wits between the man with the rod
and the fish. Manhood's men usually landed the fish. Would
I? Never. I never have done so yet. Never won a battle of
wits against a threepenny rock salmon! What am I? Fish-
head? Less than fish-head! As a child I scooped a record catch
from the Lea with a piece of sacking, my cousin holding the
other end, such a scoop that we gave half of them away,
after packing them into our jam jar and jumping on them as
the natives are reputed to do with dates.

I'm afraid that Isaak Walton, who also loved our Lea, and
often ended up his day with a flagon of ale at the Tottenham
Swan by the High Cross, would have frowned on such a
procedure. Dabbling for dace from the lacy shadow of a warm
willow, the reckless regatta of the myriad mayflies drifting
downstream, and all the rest of it, billowing cumuli and
flashing kingfisher, all those are rosy lenses in the Walton
eyeglasses. Whenever I've put them on, something drastic has
happened. The kingfisher becomes a solitary crow, very
bedraggled and squawking with hopeless complaints, the
river is grey and choppy and an East wind usurps the mayfly.
And it rains. It always rains. Jupe Pluv grows particularly
vindictive when I wandered along a river bank with rod and
line and a tin of worms. And there are never, never any fish.

Did it not invariably rain I might work up an enthusiasm for the game. The props are good. The kingfisher, the wide stream, the billowing cumuli, the willows and the water lilies, with the occasional glimpses of a vole or perhaps an otter.

Yes, the props are O.K., and were I not expected to fish I might become a votary. With bananas, beer and a book, why I grow keen already. But could you stand in thigh boots like they do in the Teviot, continually casting? Well, you'll learn your lesson when something slapstick happens to you as happened to me, and the hook catches in the seat of your trousers and you cast yourself. Not funny when you're face downwards in the river bed, though the fish manage to conceal a smile.

We had a chap at Hawick. He loved fishing, which one would think was just what he wouldn't do, his name being Jonah. A wee man of seventy odd, grizzled, like a walnut, used to poke his head in the billet. ''A' yo noo comin' fushin'?' he'd say, and Jonah would grab his tackle and go 'fushin'. That is to say, he'd stand thigh-booted in the river for two or three hours until the rain had soaked him through, and then return to the billet, pools forming wherever he stood, and tell the boys what a wonderful time he'd had, 'atishoo!' Then somebody who had already got the primus going and the pan greased ready, would ask patiently where the catch was; and on learning that there was to be no fish supper after all, would deliver a few colourful home-truths. They never discouraged Jonah however.

There was a small stage in this billet, and Jonah would perch himself on the edge of this and practise casting into the hall. He'd do that for hours with all sorts of weird and wonderful synthetic flies. Once, I'm told, though I suspect the veracity of the story, he even strewed the floor with ground bait. On reflection that may have been true, for Jonah was put away into a mental home soon after, and that was the last we saw of him and his forage cap stuck full with flies.

I had a letter from Percy's wife, Hilda, the other day. 'I am being brave,' she writes. 'No one ever broke their hearts with less fuss before. You wouldn't guess my world was in ruins when I discuss the good war news with people. You would never think that as far as I am concerned it can go on for ever and ever now.'

I promise to be very careful.

3.9.'44

Dear Spouse,

I opened a letter from you today with another twinge of annoyance. You know why, it was written in pencil. The habit is growing, so I not only chewed, I ate a whole box of Bryant and Mays to larn yer, though if anything it has 'larned' me for I've got acute bellyache. This last letter was practically invisible. The practice must stop forthwith or I volunteer for Burma. But to business. You were reading into my letter something that wasn't there, my carelessness, I'm afraid. When I said to poor Jacky Rudling: 'We've only got to keep alive for another six weeks,' I considered that the war would be over by then, not that we were due to come home. *Povero*. I'm sorry if I raised your hopes.

Rome? Well, I was never a lover of cities, and Rome didn't enthral me all that much. The best I got from it was half an hour's conversation with a woman in English. My first since we left Hawick. And making it even better, she was from Glasgow. 'I've only been out here three months, I havna' got me knees brune yet.' She worked in the Church of Scotland canteen near the Piazza Venetzia.

Now how long have you been in Maidstone? You give me little news of folk there. I hear of Maxie being browned off, being at the depot. I wish I was at the depot being browned off. I wonder if he'd really like to be back with this infantry mob? No, he reads the papers and is stirred by the advancing; so was I when I was in Rome. But the infantry is still forward. Getting stonked to hell, losing men left and right, tired, dead-beat and frightened; how it hates it. And how it is all the time wondering if it will get through this lot, if its luck will still hold, or if its wife is going to weep her heart out over a black-bordered envelope. There's none of that for you at the depot, Max, so don't be a bloody fool; realize where you are best off. Do you want to be as I am? Every time lining up for battle, and all the time looking round and thinking of all the faces that were. You know, every time I've encountered Peter Bax in the line, he's thrown his arms round me and kissed me. I'd rather you never went through the experience that prompts blokes to do that. It's unbelievable hell. Sorry, ducks, it got away with me.

Later

I have a brass plate, I shall nail it to our door and start a panel practice. Because, you see, I have passed my first-aid course with, they said, flying colours. Really it doesn't mean a thing, for to my knowledge they've yet to fail anyone. Had I failed the course and asked the reason I should have produced my sketch-book. For Assisi was a jewel of a town, tiny streets and loving craftsmanship. Not a good place to have sent me on a course with so many outside pulls!

We stayed at a large hospital, sleeping in a ward. Apart from Jenkins one night being stalked by a nightmare of the front line, and yelling out loudly in the darkness; and myself another night griped with stomach pains, and rushing up and down the corridors in bare feet, I am sleeping soundly.

You'll get my drawings eventually. Assisi is unmarked by the war. An open town, really kept so. In the church of St. Clara I saw, half revealed, a Giotto. It was whitewashed over years ago. The head of the Madonna, according to the little man who guided us, is considered the most lovely in Italy. I liked to sit on the steps of the wide *piazza* and watch the town go by, and exchange greetings with the Partisans.

But so far Rome hasn't prompted me to do a single drawing. Rome.... Rome ... and all it has meant! You think of Romans as strong rock-like people, faithful unto death. I remember the famous picture of the sentry and the falling fire of Vesuvius. Then I look at these pimps—and they are just that—they are a disgrace to the Partisans. Half of them have addresses of *signoritas* to give you. And the *signoritas*, well, I honestly think it no exaggeration to say that at least 50 per cent of them are at the game. A noisome stinking crew.

I've been knocking about with a chap named Joe Baxter. He's a mad devil with thick-lense spectacles and a smile that explodes so that suddenly his face is full of teeth. Rather like an ivory cow-catcher. Aggressive Tojo teeth. But he's mad, won the M.M. at Cassino. His old man fought in the International Brigade. Tonight I've let him go. Though he's kept with me, I feel I've had a restraining influence on him. He likes to get wildly drunk. I asked him to come to the opera. 'Oh, gosh, no!' he said. 'Tonight I want to bask on the belly of a bawdy buxom whore,' which besides being a nice line in alliteration is good round Saxon English.

Well, perhaps he basked; I shan't know until we get back, as he went before me. But not before he got me hot under the collar. It was like this. Just after the above edifying dialogue we came to a café on the junction of two main streets. 'Let's have an ice.' So we sat at a table outside, and bought ice and a drink—*vino bianca*. The ice was awful and insanitary. No cream, ice pulped and of a very dirty complexion. An old beggar woman ate them, 'Niente bonna,' we said, but she ate them just the same. She trudged on just as a flash of colour went through the door. Joe flashed spectacles and teeth in a jovial 'Bona Sera, senoreeta'. She pivoted where she stood, extending a sallow claw to the unabashed Joe. I wasn't so 'Hail sister', and she didn't shake with me. She had red finger-nails and a palimpsest of rouge on the lips. I wondered how she got her mouth open. Mebbe it didn't stick because she didn't risk shutting it.

'Wanna drink?' says Joe.

'Yes.'

At that moment a friend of the lady's joined us—yellow-skinned, and she looked tired. So there was I, sitting outside a café at the junction of one of Rome's busiest streets with two of the city's prostitutes. I didn't talk, there was no need to, for the two women were too busy comparing business and possibly discussing the immediate prospects—that being me and Joe. While I sat there a nun came up asking for alms. By then Joe and his friend were at the bar. At last I called him.

Thousands of people were going by, some—the Italians, no doubt, wondering what was wrong with the *soldat Inglisi* with the *viso molte rossa*; and the others, the troops, murmuring: 'Coo, what a couple of ol' bags.' Then as Joe returned I saw the funny side of it. The other one made no overtures in my direction. I must have looked like an elder of the Scottish Kirk. Then the ladies shook hands with us and were off. That's one thing I liked about them, they were crisp and business-like.

I left Joe Baxter and saw *I Pagliacci* at the Opera House. It was followed by the ballet *Coppelia*, which I believe is on in London—I saw pictures of it in *Picture Post*. I had an awful gallery seat (all were booked) and sweated profusely. The audience felt the heat too—the place was full of waving flags and programmes. Through my glasses I could see the Ballerina's bosom swimming with sweat. It glistened on the brows of the whole company, and likewise had a depressing effect on the costumes. They did incredibly well in such awful conditions.

11.9.'44

A woodling, doodling, pennies-down-the-well sort of letter today, for I lack substance. Do I look like an M.F.H. or possibly a rat-catcher? I was followed from breakfast by three tatterdemalion dogs this morning. They romped all the way, and when we came to the stretch of canvas under which I sleep (by the tree with the ants who apparently go to breakfast, too, for they form an incredibly long convoy right across the field—a regular Burma Road from which they never deviate) the dog with the inch-stump tail plunged into a group of turkeys, scattering them in all directions. There are grapes, and the threshing has begun. Good peasant types, and a farm I could be well content with. Four white bullocks pull the plough. Bullocks pull the cart too.

Outside the farm, at the junction of the road, is a tall cross of iron, a wayside shrine similar to many in this country. The road winds up past it, deviously as though reluctant to get to the village with the damaged church tower that crowns the hilltop. Up there, all day long, comes the sound of bells. I always think of Hemingway these days when I hear bells. It was Sunday, and a saint's day. Scruff Barton, George Pike and I had toiled up the hill. The village was still dazed from the recent impact of battle. It was quiet and sunny. Little noises carried far. The church had been damaged, a shell through the roof and a couple elsewhere. Inside, a gilded cherub sprawled perilously on a ledge. 'Look, one of those nibbos has been knocked down.'

There was a service on. The women wore black shawls, but some of the younger ones had coloured squares resting on their heads. There were men and babes, too. We came out, sat on some steps and I sketched the scene. As I said, it was a saint's day, and apparently one had to get there even if it meant leaving the most pressing housework. But it need only be for a minute or so; there were women hurrying in and out all the time.

A man in a black gown came out with a censer, clumped up the road, up the steps on which we sat, and into the house. Meanwhile, from this battered church came some wonderful singing. On the calm evening air it sounded perfect.

The Italians have no less curiosity than the English, and anybody drawing soon gets a crowd. Soon we were talking with folk, and after a while it occurred to me that shots of the English out here talking to the Italians would make quite an amusing newsreel, on account of the tremendous amount of mime necessary. I, for instance, had to mount an imaginary motor-bike, while a man in the infantry taps his boots and says with lessening patience: You know—*infantry*—plates of meat!'

Later we spoke with two of the churchmen. One could write English better than he spoke it, and showed us a sheet he'd typed, asking the military for assistance in rebuilding the church.

The New Statesman is arriving regularly, and makes my best reading nowadays, though no one would call this reading extensive. It's often limited, for weeks at a time, to dropped pamphlets when we're in the line, to the detail board when we're out of it.

28.9.'44

I don't have to worry about Joe Baxter any more. Jerry was coming along the road and Joe, brave and wild as ever, leapt up and confronted them alone. Whether he got any first I don't know, but he was filled with bullets in no time. He was idolized by his company, and you may remember won the M.M. at Cassino. He was full of plans for the post-war world. I was shocked by the news, though always expecting it.

I am very glad that my brother Ben was taken prisoner. Glad, too, that Jack Steel and the others were also, for they would have to have had my luck to escape Joe's fate. Who shall condemn Joe Baxter for his actions in Rome? 'Wine and women while we've got the chance,' inevitably becomes the philosophy of hundreds of soldiers. It is understandable enough. I have not embraced it, but I am affected in other ways. My remarks about Maxie was evidence of it. Much of what I wrote about Maxie that upset you still holds, but I realized I was a bit severe, and my very next letter was written to Maxie telling him about it and asking him to try and understand. Now I must ask you to do the same thing.

I have told you a few things since I left Hawick, but they have been only a tiny part of the whole. I have never told you of the worst things. To be doing a guy up, and to have him biting your trousers in agony, and then to have him die on the stretcher on the way back, that's enough; but it's nothing. I've told you nothing of the really grisly and horrific things, and I won't; but you'd understand more if I did. And I'm not really losing my sense of proportion, but I am weary and sickened of seeing the Percys, the Jacky Rudlings, and the Joe Baxters go one after the other. I want to see Chopper and Steve and Buff, and the few that are left, out of it, myself too; instead of going on flouting all the time the terrible law of averages, which I fear will one day assert itself.

We are now floundering about, ankle-deep in mud, and the prospect draws nearer, of a bitter hard-fighting winter. We have moved, and I no longer boast a studio. I am in the Company Office at the moment, a largish tent, my boots embellished by scalloped and very glutinous mud.

I received a book of cartoons yesterday. I wish that occasionally you would send me a good literary book. I don't want to sound unappreciative of the cartoon book, but I'd like some good reading, not fiction—in fact, one on writing and English literature would fill the bill at the moment. The candle's wobbling—good night.

3.10.'44

Dear Wife,

Winter warfare here is going to be pretty sticky. It's not winter yet, but the landscape is soggy and puddled, and it rains every other day. Roads are few. The ways are largely tracks across fields. The skies weep and weep and weep. It is often cold, and once one is wet there is little chance of drying out. 'Don't put those things on yet,' my mother used to say, 'they're not aired yet.' She ought to see some of those things now. Fortunately we are in a house, but what the conditions are like in the front line slit trenches I shiver to imagine, it gives me mental pneumonia. There'll be crocks from rheumatics alone after the war.

There's no sign of autumn yet. It is summer one week and, click, you're pitchforked into mid-winter weather. There are no autumn tints, but the rain-filled fields are full of seared stalks of maize, a spectacle even more cheerless than hopfields in winter. And I never slipped and sploshed in such mud in all my life. All the time the Italians are wandering back to shattered homes, looking over the wrecks of their houses. Many go barefoot.

I had another trip to Arezzo last week, to bring back four deserters. While there I went to see the famous frescoes by Piero di Francesca, only to find a stout wall had been built in front of them for protection. I visited Monte San Savino, and Percy's grave in a little cemetery with about forty of our men in. White crosses marking fallen West Kents are sprinkled all over this country. Past Assisi and into Spillo, which is the village in which I had my 'studio'.

138

I called on friends, and it was demonstrated once again what good ambassadors the boys with the rampant horse are. Our little truck was mobbed, and later, as I was walking through a square, one woman, apparently posted as look-out in a doorway, turned and jabbered something to people inside, whereupon there was an excited exodus and I was dragged in by a dozen hands. Then I was shown photos of the boys, and questioned as to the welfare of all these *amigis*. 'Si si, tutti bene, tutti bene.' All are well. And would I take notes? No correspondence is allowed between us and civvies, but I agreed, whereupon much hasty writing followed. I was plied with drink, and had I accepted it all, I wouldn't be recovered yet. My driver and two escorts were elsewhere, and when we found them we were given more drinks and invited to eat. When I said that we had to get away they gave me something to eat in the truck. This was half a brown loaf which had been hollowed out and filled with gobbets of rabbit fried in olive oil and tomato juice. I heartily recommend it. It was gorgeous. I honestly don't remember when I enjoyed anything as much as those bits of rabbit. You must try your hand at it.

Of the war, Hermy says: 'We take the last ridge before the plains; it rains, washes all the mud away, and in the morning there's another ridge to fight for.' I saw a house on the skyline today, and silhouetted on the top floor I could see an old woman searching among the ruins of her bedroom. It was easy to see her, she was framed by great gaps in the front and side wall. A tank was rusting in the foreground. Such a scene raises no comment here. And it's the same all over the world. Shrug the shoulders, 'c'est la guerre'. That's all. Our senses and sympathies can't comprehend too much. They were numbed a long time ago, I suppose. A train or the *Thetis* disaster could shake the world once. Now refugees are a nuisance. There's a great deal more than homes and cities for us to reconstruct.

16.10.'44

The 'phone buzzes (I am in the same room as our 3 Coy. Signals) and I get the following requests throughout the day: (*a*) Would I accept a commission to draw D Coy.'s village for Major B. (They had quite an exciting scrap there—a Custer's last stand sort of thing—except that they came off top. Buffin was in a house there at the time and says he dived under a bed so hard that he jammed his helmet on to his head.) (*b*) Would I paint a Company sign for Charley Coy. (*c*) Major Reeves says can I get another casualty fund letter done today. (*d*) Would I come round to Charley and paint the back of Lt. M.'s neck to resemble a face as he's doing an act at a concert tonight. And then Lt. McG., a New Zealander, comes up and asks would I do his portrait on an air-letter to send home as an Xmas greeting! You see that I am excusing myself for not being able to write to you for some days.

Enough perhaps; but conditions here are awful, too, and for the Italians perhaps worse. They all sleep in a stable, something like thirty of them, *bambinos* as well—and two oxen. Not unnaturally it stinks, and there are many ill as well. *Bambinos* swarming about the place are always needing treatment for sores, cuts and so on. One poor kid caught the splutterings of part of a phosphorus bomb—which have a nasty boring, burning action. Then we had two people with temperatures of over a hundred. The Doc. has been swamped with civilian patients from all around, and has been too busy to get round. Treating these people in the dingy and stinking stables with civilians worrying you with questions is quite a headache. But I got a bigger one when four went down in one day.

Picture the scene. Mattresses and blankets on the straw. Two or three in a bed. Little kids in dim mangers. I went round to see the Doc. I feared an epidemic in such conditions. The people who were sick were sweating profusely, had occasional nose bleeds and ran consistently high temperatures. First it looked like malaria, but the symptoms weren't consistent; it developed into typhoid! Phew! What a flap. Evacuate them at once, check up on our inoculations, and impose strict supervision of all water used. And now cases are reported from the surrounding area. You see why I have been unable to write. My time out of the line is every bit as busy as my time in it—though it has never been at its present pressure. Having caught those people at an early stage there is no danger of a widespread epidemic, in fact, a period of quarantine is not necessary.

Interval here. I've been to bring in another typhoid case. A woman of fifty-six, who looked eighty. Poor Papa was crying, both were wizened, gnarled and seamed. I should say he'd never see Mamma again. We helped her down the stairs—there were two sheep in the lower room—and lifted her into the jeep. It's all very depressing. These poor people, all their lives struggling against the land and poverty. Papa's hopeless snivelling. Oh dear, it's all so pathetic. And they are perforce treated in the most perfunctory way. They all want to accompany the various patients and it's just not possible. It's extremely unlikely they would ever be able to make their way to the hospital, or would be allowed to see their relations if they did. It seems so hopeless for them.

20.10.'44

You know the story of Persephone, how she goes into the earth for six months and reappears again in the spring. Well, my boots are like that. And yesterday I went down to C Coy. (where they have a gramophone) in the ambulance jeep. We went by way of a track across the fields. The wheels hardly gripped, but we got there, skidding and slithering down the slopes, often nearly broadside on. Tony Marchant, who sends his love (he used to kiss your photograph when we were up in the mountains and I wasn't looking), had scrounged some records from Corps, and in that dingy room with a dingy candle we played the Unfinished, and Beethoven's Fifth, and one or two more. Later in a barn-like room below, mud-died with the tramp of boots, and evil-smelling because the rain had stirred up the cesspool just outside the door, and likewise dim and dingy, we had a do-as-you-please concert.

A few weeks ago forty-two German prisoners crowded this room, all shapes and all sizes. Now Chopper came up from 'A' Coy., wearing a trilby hat dripping from the eaves. There was a demand for the Cassino song, a parody I wrote in honour of the porters who brought the food and ammo up, but he wouldn't sing it, as I knew he wouldn't for Percy was always singing it. But he sang some good numbers in the one and only Chopper style; and while he sang I kept remembering how Tony had talked with the German prisoners, one a little bespectacled stretcher bearer.

Later, I slept on a stretcher in the 'concert hall'. Blokes were sleeping all along the walls. Bunny and Percy Childs and Fish were in one bed with a mattress and a yellow quilt, while Tony and George, the two biggest lads in the battalion, shared a single bed. Not all had beds, most kipped on the floor. But with so many crippled houses about mattresses are not uncommon.

I have been considering sending a cartoon to the *Kent Messenger*, but again circumstances sit tight on time. Too facile with excuses you say? Well, consider that it's dark at seven these days, and we usually have about one candle amongst about eight men. We're billeted in this farmhouse, beset with mud. The Italian family cooks on a wood fire below, and a big sheet of tarpaulin is stretched across the table to catch the leaks in the war-torn roof. The kids are all barefooted, I saw one yesterday paddling in the centre of the room. A middle-aged woman rolls the spaghetti, it looks like the flat motsa that Jews eat at this stage, she rolls the spaghetti and breaks wind. They all sleep in the ox-manger, it stinks horribly. When we went down to dress some sores this morning a tiny curly-haired tot was squatting among the straw, gurgling away.

The battle has rolled on, but the land is eloquent. There is an upturned carrier by a farmhouse, new crosses mark the graves of our boys, and many an 'unknown German soldier'. Scattered about is German ammunition.

Yesterday a wounded boy came in here. We got his story and made our way hastily to another lone house on the skyline. There we found a wailing family washing and laying out a little boy of nine. The bastard who set that booby trap ought to get a lot of satisfaction out of it. And that sort of thing will go on, and the world will say: 'What's on at the Odeon this week?'

23.10.'44

To say that I write this under trying circumstances is an understatement, as was Churchill's 'soft under-belly'. Exactly what the circumstances are I am nowise permitted to say at this juncture, but in due course you shall know. You may then think back, and try and work out what you were doing yourself at this time. I always wonder. Sometimes, for instance, when you are all snuggled up to the chin under fleecy blankets and expressing a hope that I am as comfortable, it may, and certainly often has been, far different. I have at those very moments been running the terrible gauntlet of hostile shelling with a chap on a stretcher. There is no sound more sickening than German artillery, none more heartening than Allied. Mortars, heavy artillery, and the banshee *nebelwurfers* are merciless. They smack the ground and give the impression of great iron hands spanking the ground with overlapping spanks. Spanks which tremble the earth for an acre around and under which you would think nothing could survive. It is fiercer out here than anything we encountered in North Africa, and we thought nothing could be worse than that.

These days my command of three has changed in personnel. My three 'Cossacks'—amiable Jimmy Fevin, stolid pipe-smoking Mitchell, and loud-mouthed, garish but none the less likeable Wally—have ceded to another three. Jimmy is in dock with a groggy knee, while the other two are resting. Now I have a more elderly crew. Joe, from Poplar, doesn't smoke or drink, gets twelve letters a day and writes twenty, he has been for fifteen years a St. John's ambulance man. He is very useful and appears to like dealing with the wounded, whereas I have to conquer a certain revulsion, being afraid, as I cut the clothing, what I shall find. There's an awful sickening smell about a wound, and we often get smothered with blood, so that the flies gravitate towards one in droves. My next man is grey-haired Jack from Watford, one-time plumber. A nice chap with a high-pitched bomb-happy laugh, which may be just what it is, though his conduct is always good and reliable in battle. He was for a long time a rifleman in 'A' Company and was one of the few who answered the call for volunteers for the depleted stretcher bearers. He may be a little better off, out of the line, since we are not pestered like the riflemen are; but some consider that he has fallen out of the frying-pan into the fire. (Personally, I don't envy the company rifleman his job, I think it is the worst in the world.) Anyway, Jack from Watford, who has a wife and a babe, is good and steady. My next one is another Somerset boy from the next village to Jimmy Fevin. He is short, sturdy and muddy, very broad in his speech. And for a long time I couldn't cotton on to what he was saying. 'Everything 'appens to 'oi,' is his favourite saying. He is comical, always good humoured and has inexhaustible energy, always on the go. A feature of his, as natural as his nose, is his billy-can, and his welcome habit of brewing up at every opportunity. He's a good boy, and does so many things for me that I grow embarrassed and ask him not to, though he's the same with everybody else. He has a way of getting on with Italians, too. At our last place one of the loveliest girls I've ever seen came up and posed for me. Andy, who was smaller than she, just planted himself stolidly in front of her, gazed up at her and said: 'Golly, but you're beautiful.' I've seen few things that were so comical. One thing about girls here, they always pose willingly. 'Andy, I'd like a model,' I say. He goes, he comes back, genie-like, and a model is with him. How he explains it to them I don't know, only they seem to understand his burring Somerset much more easily than my halting Italian. And they all like Andy. You would too. By the way, she was very beautiful, but only a model!

27.10.'44

On the day which I believe was your birthday we liberated several square miles. I told the boys what day it was and they made a special effort. The Italians we came across were so joyous that I think someone had told them also. 'Inglisi! Inglisi!' enthused one old boy, scooping up dirt and letting it fall over him as utility confetti. And Buff's company were met on one occasion by women who rushed forward and embraced them, whereupon Bruno moved well into the vanguard so that he could meet their embraces and reciprocate heartily. Just in his line. Poor old Tony got his second Purple Heart, however. One of our tanks had blundered blindly over a slit trench and buried two of the boys in it. Joe and I dug frenziedly for an hour, under cover of our Red Cross flag—a sniper with a Spandau had been zipping bursts of tracer across—and eventually we got Bradley out. His mate was dead, suffocated. Bradley was saved by the fact that a slab of brickwork had pressed on his helmet and allowed air to get through. I put a rifle sling round this lump of masonry and had to call on two fellows before I could shift it. Bradley was O.K., so we left him to get back in his own time, and went in pursuit of our company.

We met 'C' Company all the way, did them up and eventually ran across Tony lying by himself in an orchard. He waved wearily, and propped there on an elbow managed a smile. 'Hallo, you bloody fool, you copped it again?' 'Yeah,' he sounded disgusted, 'don't leave me will you.' Our own tanks again; in the confusion they had been firing on our own men. Tony, who has got bags of guts, tried to signal by raising the stretcher. This, of course, entailed getting up, and Tony caught a burst through both legs, one being a fractured femur.

His wounds had been worked on by Percy Childs—lying flat under the bullets—but Percy was now gone to a nearby house to salvage some bedding to tear up in strips for splint binding. Bits of barrel wood were already loosely applied to the fracture, but there was no binding material about. We tried to get him on the stretcher, two of us, Tony putting his arms round Joe's neck—Joe straddled the stretcher—and I supported the broken limb. But Tony is six foot and a colossal weight, we could hardly shift him; the effort, abortive though it was, set poor Tony trembling, and the sweat starting in great beads on his forehead. He bit his lips and clenched his hands against the pain. 'Sorry, Robbie,' he said. 'Don't know what Maggie Gunn would say.'

Somehow that's like a present for you. A badly wounded man in an Italian orchard and likely to be the centre of an enemy stonk at any moment, thinking of you. I gave him a shot of morphia in the arm. Percy Childs returned with the sheeting and his mate Bunny, and in half an hour we had the leg fixed up. Then, because of Tony's vast stature and corresponding weight, and the difficulty of lifting him on to the stretcher, he had to be more or less slid on to it. The wretched bottom piece of the splint got caught under the stretcher. We cut the stretcher a bit, but even so it caused pain that might have been avoided. But Tony was good. We got him into a ruined house. Three other wounded were there, one with a bullet in his spine. He just lay there under a blanket, on his side. 'Hallo, Robbie,' he said. 'Hallo, Bas, how d'you feel?' 'Bit dodgy like.' 'Never mind, I've got a shot of morphia for you here.'

We were leaving wounded here and there in the wake of the battle. They would be picked up later by jeep. We couldn't take them back at this stage as we had to be up with the battle. We left Bunny and Percy with Tony. His will be a long job, fourteen months the Doc. reckons, and almost certainly a shortened leg at the end of it. He's such a grand physical specimen, too. We shook hands and he said: 'Tell Maggie Gunn that I still love her and still kiss her photograph.' He's got that one we used to have in the mountains, the one marked with chocolate where we used to kiss it in unfailing ritual, morning and night. I'd like you to go and see him when he gets to England.

We had to cross a river under shell-fire—wading it in the dead of night. Navel-deep until we trod in a shell hole, when the water came up to the chest. I thought of you getting ready for your birthday celebrations, and wished I could share them instead of going about in wet things with no possibility of changing them. And then it rained. The bridgehead was pretty precarious and the shelling the heaviest we had encountered. My pack, mess-tin and towel were riddled with shrapnel. Fortunately, when that one landed, I was away with a casualty and had left the pack in my trench. My sketch-book, too, was safe, still tied to the top of my helmet, where I had put it prior to the river crossing.

A battle followed and that night I spent in a house, expecting a counter-attack, and having the dickens of a job to check the bleeding from a leg wound sustained by one of the five wounded in the house. These men couldn't get back because at that time all attempts to throw a bridge over the river were shelled to hell. So they lay there in their wet clothes. We couldn't show a light except a screened torch or candle. Then, while some of the others risked sleep, for they were dog-tired, I managed something of which I am inordinately proud. I brewed up on a candle. Wrapped it round with bandages and boiled half a mess-tin, just enough to make tea for the casualties. It is a tramp's job, and among my former brethren of the road is known as 'dollying-up'. Another wrinkle: I dried wet matches in my hair. They are O.K. after a minute or two.

Next day we got the wounded down to the river. It was rising, and extremely swift. We got them over to the ambulance by boat. The current swung the boat down the river, we had a hefty long pull on the ropes. Those casualties must have felt 100 per cent better on the other side. Just before crossing the river some mail was brought up. Three paint brushes for me! Someone else got income tax papers!

4.11.'44

I'm excited! Like a man liberated! We're starting a Divisional newspaper, and I am sub-editor! What does that mean? It means, my love, that the days of your anxiety and mine

are over! It means that I am permanently at Division and
have crawled from my last muddy slit trench. It means that
I shall be out of Spandau, mortar and most shelling range.
And at the same time do a job perhaps more vital in the fight
against Fascism.

The editorial staff seems to be only myself and a captain,
and we have six on the printing side. We aim to appear next
week, but haven't enough type at the moment. The skipper
and comp. are away to Florence, scrounging it. Also they are
trying to find block-makers for cartoons. Too bad if they
don't succeed. What a sub-editor has to do I don't exactly
know, but since we will now be permitted to live, we will
doubtless learn. And you can help. If I am permitted to do so
(there is some doubt), I will send you the first copy—my
purple passages and all. Criticize, but criticize fairly. And keep
me supplied with books. Books of fact, books on English,
good writing, common grammatical errors and so on. And
a shorthand, mine has rusted on me. It is important too that
I have sport books, reference annuals, football handbooks. I'll
send the money.

I got here by virtue of a good build-up by the C.O. So
here I am at a desk, with good lighting, a fire, and generally
so happily situated that when I think of Steve, Buff, Chopper
and the boys I feel a heel. They all wished me well, however.
Mind you, I'm busy, working until twelve the last two nights,
with as yet little to show for it. But we'll shake down soon.
And it's good work. Keep me up to it culturally, I'm not in
my best form, you know. I need mental convalescence and
rehabilitation. This might do the trick, but I must not dodge
solid reading, as I have been doing lately.

One other important thing: I want lino-cutting tools and

even lino, for out here, though we are searching for it, we have small hope of finding any, as all the floors are tiled. These are for immediate illustration purposes for such stuff as cannot stand a journey to Florence and back or wherever it is we might be getting blocks made. Wish me luck, my love.

11.11.'44

I look out of the door of this office and see two drooping ponies, two carts, and a black-bearded monk lifting a box from one of them. He has a brown habit and a black skull-cap not unlike a Juliet cap. There are cobbles, and now one pony has pulled out with a slow clip-clop, the monk has gone with it and an army three-tonner has pulled across the door-way and is blocking my view. People are still drifting back, still drifting sadly about the tumbled rubble of what was once their homes. They are everywhere attempting repairs. I saw a woman throwing tiles from a balcony to her husband who was perched among the bared ribs of the roof. I saw a nun holding a ladder for a grizzled old boy struggling with the bulging shutters of a shop. Civilians are shovelling at the huge pyramids of fallen masonry and getting it away in lorries. A lone length of guttering dangles precariously from a 'phone wire in a narrow, many-arched street near the Piazza del Populo.

An old beldame came in this morning begging for bread. In dusty black she was, as though she had just crept from some bomb-wrack. Jock, who is from Aberdeen and a rich charac-ter, said: 'Sit thee doon momma and hae some tay.' 'Grazie,' and she warmed her poor old claws round the mug. She had exactly two teeth, long, yellow and loose. I saw the poor old soul this afternoon as I wandered down by the river. She was pushing a little handcart and gabbling shrilly at three boys. She turned in among the tumbled chaos of what was once a home. I wondered if it was hers. Her plight is like that of many who patch up broken walls against the oncoming winter, who crowd round the Amgot place for permits and work, whose prospect for the coming season is pretty bleak.

There is shocking, widespread, and saddening devastation down by the river. The bridge is still magnificent in its ruin. There is a Bailey bridge over the blown gap, and the figures on it and the transport stand clear against the sky. Its arches are among the noblest I have ever seen. But how did anyone live near? There's not an ant could have survived that bombardment, you'd think. I waded this river at midnight under shell fire, I followed Bill Teal with a big 18 set balanced on his head. It scared me this afternoon just to look at it!

I heard the radio gaff about V 2 last night. Any near ones? They scoffed at them, but I can't help wondering.

The editor is still away collecting type and stuff, so the first issue of the paper has yet to appear. Meanwhile I'm in command of the office and have been collecting local news. I interviewed Miss Gabrielle Brune, who is here for a week at the opera house. I asked her what her ambition was. She thought a bit and said: 'To go home and lie down!'

There is snow on the hills between here and Rome. We've felt it in the air all day—and there is no glass in our windows. And there are boys in the slit trenches . . .

I'll write you an overdue letter. I must first warn you about premature whoopings over the paper. It has yet to be given the O.K. We in the printing office have the first issue ready, but it is subject to the approval of people of all kinds save those whom we expect to be catering for, namely, the boys in the slit trenches. Nothing sterner than a b—— can be used in the way of the more common and forceful kind of army language; we have, in fact, to gang warily a' the time. What will happen if this initial issue of the *Quadrant* meets with a frown from the divisional up-tops I don't know. Possibly the whole project will be scrapped, more probably a fresh staff of near-choirboys will be engaged. Therefore I say hold your whoops, and be content with merely crossing your fingers. As it is I am rather disappointed with No. 1, Vol. 1, but as there have been many teething troubles it is not surprising perhaps that the present complexion is a little pimply.

It falls to me to do quite a bit of cartooning, and yesterday found me with a list of appointments so that by the end of the day I had drawn a Lt.-General, a full Colonel, three Lt.-Colonels, and a jeep driver! The snag is that I am very conscious of the fact that these boys have a war on their hands, and I am therefore not fully at ease. However, without exception I find these big and biggerwigs mighty charming and accommodating people. The General fixed the light for me, expressed great surprise at the rapidity of my work, and was altogether as nice as pie. Another snag is that these people are so rarely seen by the rank and file—to which I belong—that one does not know those mannerisms or idiosyncrasies which are essential for caricature. Have I sufficiently dampened your enthusiasm? Right, so now let me tell you that I think we will pull through!

27.11.'44

Dear Wife,

I always fancy that I construe better when using a type-writer, so when you see me using a pen you can deduce that no typewriter is to hand. And from that you might, in this case, deduce something else, for since no newspaper office is without its typewriter, it might on some occasions follow, conversely, that no typewriter meant no newspaper office. And in this instance the deduction would be correct. There is no newspaper office, nor even a newspaper. Ah me! Such hopes too. But it was something quite outside our power, something which in the fullness of time you will know, but which for security reasons, I am not at liberty to divulge at the moment. It was from no reasons of personal inefficiency, the suspension is no reflection on the staff.

Suspension, you'll notice. For that's all it is. The trouble is that such a lot can happen between now and the day of resumption and it may well be that the retainer we have at the moment may be no longer valid in new circumstances. Meanwhile, we are to be returned to our units with the promise that when the paper gets going again we'll be with it.

A sad disappointment, particularly as No. 1, which we produced in restricted supply, has been approved of by all the boys who have seen it. I am fairly optimistic, it takes buckets to dampen me, about the *Quadrant* restarting though, for with print and paper bought, a machine fixed in a lorry, it's unlikely that the project will fall by the wayside. In the meantime I can polish: which means brushing up shorthand, facing all those parliamentary bills I have been avoiding, caricaturing, and trying to enlarge a mind which I have felt to be more and more circumscribed with the adding up of battles and the weary months of war, and increasingly loath to explore on its own account. Good night.

16.12.'44

Any woman in parlous circumstances moves me to compassion, and sometimes to rage against the colossal powers ranged against the improvement of her lot. This is true whether she be a gnarled old beldame searching the black mountain side for kindling, or an ugly frumpish peasant girl with wind-coarsened skin and blunt hands. But when it is beauty one sees so struggling, it saddens me still more. The tragedy of beauty is no greater than the tragedy of the frumpish, and the greater pity comes, I suppose, from a basis of sex and masculine desire. However it is, the woman who so moved me was lovely, past her best, but still shining by force of her dark and melancholy beauty against a background of merciless poverty. Her home was squalid, one of many such homes sprawled at the foot of the mountains. 'It is the life they are used to, they are content because they know no other,' say the boys. Mebbe, but a life of drudgery, a life of losing struggle is no life for anybody, less still for a woman, less still for a beautiful woman with sad black eyes, a quiet dignity and melancholy grace. Anna and Pepita, her two children, are beautiful too, but what hue is on their cheeks now—little enough—would pale overnight were they to realize that their heritage was to be the same hard lot that was their mother's.

She was worried, half-frightened of us when we first came in, but she is more at ease now. When there is no common language, apart from a hotch-potch of Italian, German, Greek and English, one relies chiefly on little gifts, but with soap, chocolate, and matches hard to come by, that isn't so easy. The pencil helped with a sketch of Grandpa and another of Grandma in a black cowl spinning wool off a sort of shepherd's crook and bobbin. So now she knows there is nothing to fear. She opened the parlour for Killer Gorman and me, and we slept on a worn carpet, but it snowed in the night and water splashed through the roof in large drops. We are here a second time, having left for three days when the company went as protection to the Engineers building a bridge over the gorge. I thought about the living-room—a bed in it and a square black stove making a chimney through the wall like a gun, and I thought of the unavailing struggle to clothe the family and to keep down dirt. Someone ought to wave a wand, I said, and transform her rags to lovely gowns, and she should dance and laugh and punt down the river. She is the beginning of all fairy tales. But her story has lingered too long in chapter one, leaving her scratching her scabies. The book doesn't say so, but I suspect that Cinderella had scabies. We call her Cinderella. She scratches furtively, but Anna and Pepita scratch with less reserve, lifting their clothes, clawing their stomachs and wriggling them against their hands to scratch the more vehemently.

The mountain is capped with snow, and today in the thaw the village is a thousand rushing streams of brown. There is every sort of sound that water can make: drips, splashes, gurgles, oozes and squelches; streams, pools and puddles and, the rapid drip, drip, dripping from roof gutters. And there is not one pair of warm feet in the community. I should say that 80 per cent of the folk in this village have scabies. We shall probably get it too, particularly as our circumstances are such that we've had no change of underwear for weeks. Don't worry, the cure is effected in forty-eight hours. But I would love a bath—a long sit-down one—and a change into clean clothes.

1944-5
GREECE

⟨§§§⟩

Dear Lass,

One day a caterpillar was pursuing its corrugated way along the back of an elephant who was crossing a stream. Halfway along it met a starling. 'Shoot,' it cried to friends on the bank. 'Shoot the elephant.' The friends obeyed, and both elephant and caterpillar fell into the stream and were drowned. Not very good that, but in the front line we have difficulty in seeing the whole, we are so close that we are cross-eyed. The caterpillar cannot see the elephant. So it is here. We, dear one, are in ancient, classic and tragic Greece. In a position which is as unhappy and distressing as it is difficult to understand. Only if one knows the historic background of these situations can one hope to understand what is going on. Here we have a smaller knowledge of facts than ever before, and no one so far has attempted to give a picture of the politics from which this crisis arose.

The first word to greet us on our arrival in Athens was 'Shell', and from various words we encountered—particularly those painted on the walls—we got an inkling of the origins and various stages of the struggle here. One sees 'Welcome brave Englishmen'—to greet the army of General Scobie—and the greeting is from all parties. But predominant is the red paint of E.A.M., E.L.A.S. and K.K.E. The walls bear something more than slogans. They are more like newspapers, bearing messages anything from four to a hundred words in length, all, of course, in Greek. The mural press situation, from a growing lack of unused space, must have been such as to demand the attention of a sub-editor by the time we arrived. I haven't noticed a clear wall yet. They're crammed with writing. Houses by the hundred have huge Hammers and Sickles painted centrally over the door, and, if there are pillars, something is there too. We are in a school at the moment, a day or so ago occupied by the E.L.A.S., and containing, when we came in, lots of bloodstained rags and dressings.

Some of our men were helping to feed the people yesterday. Troops trying to organize the crowd, allowing pregnant women priority—a new job for the troops, that, combing the crowds for signs of pregnancy. They were, I understand, in the position of minor Canutes, for the people stampeded the counter. One barefoot boy was brought in with badly bruised feet where people had trodden on him. They got dry rations here, bread, tea, etc. There have been soup kitchens, too.

While all this was going on, tracer bullets were skimming the roof-tops about three hundred yards away. It's not easy to imagine a city engaged in fratricidal warfare. It might be a game of tennis that goes on, when Greek meets Greek, to judge by the behaviour of the other citizens. Even quite near to the fighting kids will be playing, women hanging washing out, and a vendor will be pushing a barrow up the street, selling figs. Where he is going goodness knows, but you feel he would go on unperturbed by bullets and mortar bombs, and would continue right through the lethal criss-cross of bullets in no-man's-land if he thought he'd get another customer.

No one is allowed out without armed escort, so I accompanied the Padre in a little constitutional yesterday. We went into a church, the Padre hoping to be able to arrange a service. Soon we were hobnobbing with six of the priests of the Greek Orthodox Church, with their black gowns, chimney hats and black beards; but only the caretaker could speak English, and that of the American variety.

The streets hereabouts have a spacious, shall I say North Harrow look. There seems to be no strongly nationalist type of building as we saw in Italy. Delivered blindfolded here, you would need several guesses before you guessed where you were. The pavements are hard and dry and a bleak wind flurries the trees. People step briskly. It will be a frugal Christmas here, but I would be well content with my biscuits and eternal stew if only an amicable settlement of the trouble were arrived at.

3.1.'45

The other day I helped to feed the starving populace. In a pitifully squalid district. It was a cold and crisp morning and the wind was spiteful. I shivered in a greatcoat and jerkin; how the poorly shod and underfed Greeks stood it, is something at which I still marvel. There were four queues, the men's; the women and girls; old men; and the one I was in charge of—old ladies and expectant mothers. For hours they stood, unavailing scarves wrapped across their mouths and over their heads. There were often rushes for the gates of the school where the stuff was being dispensed, but after a while, by dint of my most persuasive manner, I had achieved a patient and orderly line. There is much to be said for the butt-of-the-rifle or horsewhip method, for persuasiveness let me in for a lot of wheedling stories. Every now and then an old mother would break the line to come up and give me a long story. Many mothers, faces brown and wrinkled as raisins, dear old souls, were resorting to arch smiles and rusty graces to wheedle round me. The pregnant women who go through first were subjected to an examination by a woman of the feeding staff. This took place in the middle of the road, the expectant one drawing back her coat while her stomach was felt for cushions. That trick has been pulled once or twice. All this lining up was for a small bag of white beans. There had been soup powder, but that didn't last long. The organization wasn't what you would call fluent, and if E.L.A.S. fired a shot in the vicinity no food would be issued for twenty-four hours. There are not the spindly legs and distended stomachs I expected here, and which is symptomatic of Indian famines. I wonder why the difference. I should say that the Indians are dragged down with dysentery, malaria and all the rest of it. These people are not affected in the same way physically, though their constitutional resistance is probably no better than that of the Indians. The decline will be imperceptible, but collapse will come, the more sudden for that. They'll drop in the streets, a collapse rather than wilting.

We've been among the poorer classes, and they seem to subsist on a hard nut like a Spanish nut, which they bake to ball-bearing hardness. Yet the shops were full in Athens when the first troops landed. The prices were way up in the stratosphere. A bar of chocolate is sold for half a crown. The market places have a fair number of stalls with an array of food, but it must be black market. I don't know why it is tolerated. I suppose the average price of a small tin of corned beef is fifteen shillings—with many fluctuations.

The people in our first district were quite well dressed, but here many of the kids go barefooted, and it's quite cold weather. Where we fed the people that day civilians were sawing up the kerbside trees. We've had some rain, but nothing like the Italian amount, and I understand that dry weather obtains most of the year.

Some good news. Hermy and Tony have both been awarded the M.M. while the old Doc. got the M.C. All richly deserved.

By the way, don't be too optimistic about the prospect of leave, this business seems to have gummed up the works a bit.

10.1.'45

They laughed when they recalled the game with the other English soldiers, and how black the face of one of them had been from burnt cork because he had been left with the Queen and lost. He was rather stupid, Costa explained, he had been caught every time. I took my pick and the game proceeded; three games proceeded, and at the end of them I had one black cross marking my forehead and two on my cheeks. I laughed uncomfortably.

This was in a billet in Athens. Costa spoke English rather well, having been a year in America studying engineering. He had also had eight years studying in Turkey. The house was modest, and shared with his sister and a girl called Jane and her brother. He was thickly spectacled, thickly jowled and thickly necked. He was very hairy and very black. He looked rather like the spirit of coal just back from a long journey through sooty chimneys. He had a bandage round his neck where shrapnel had skimmed it. It was Jane day when we first got to the house. Birthdays are not celebrated here. Instead every day is a name day, and if it is your name day your friends will call expecting a traditional piece of cake and wine, and often it means a party. Jane day was also John day and in the afternoon a friend called and took the two men to visit a John they knew. For poor Jane it was no day for high spirits. She wore a dressing-gown all day because all her clothes had been burnt in another house. She mourned them silently all day long. She forgot them only when we began cheating at Newmarket and half the company were on their feet, watching the dealer.

Costa said that he could not work under the Germans. So he sold a house and some land and contrived to live on the proceeds. Today he is shabby and the soles of his shoes ring-wormed with long service. But many people did accept work under the Germans, and it is just these people, Costa complained, who are getting work now.

19.1.'45

All day long the snow fell soft and silently, muffling the mountains and muting the village. That was yesterday, and we saw another crazy aspect of the war, for it was the third day of the truce and the village was crowded with E.L.A.S. We shook hands with the 'enemy' and gave them smokes. They were a tatterdemalion crew, and picturesque, some of them with black Cossack hats of fur, others in German Afrika Corps uniform, a few in British, or in Italian, but most in oddments of several or all of these uniforms. Many were in civvies, and one wore a heavy monkish garment of rough fur like a bear-skin, highly cowled and all-enveloping.

There was as strange a mixture of weapons, Tommy guns, Italian Bredas, German stick bombs, and a three-inch mortar carried by a shaggy pony. Ages ranged from fourteen to

forty. I was told that one or two girls were there, but being
in masculine attire I did not see them as they went by. It was
a company going through, and though some of them were
dreadfully tattered it did not prevent them playing snowballs
during their wait in the village. One or two were barefooted.
They produced a case of corned beef and began to eat. Village
women, wives and relations, came down and spoke with the
men.

It was not surprising that our reception wasn't a warm one
here. We soon found an interpreter who could speak English
and one of our captains, the Sergeant-Major, some of the
boys and myself held quite a pow-wow with the chap, and an
E.L.A.S. officer. We realized then that E.L.A.S. wasn't just
the rabble and hooligan band we had been told it was. The
man who spoke English surprised us all with his grasp of
things.

We saw how an atrocity story can start. We were in a
house when one of our fellows came in calling for stretcher
bearers. 'A woman's had her eye cut out by E.L.A.S.,' he
said. But when I went out, two chaps were struggling across
the road with the casualty, a man! And he was stinking of
meths., drunk. He had fallen on a rail. This was the woman
with the eye cut out by E.L.A.S.

The damage had been done by then. Fellows had heard the
story and passed it on before the truth had been established.
They will relate the story as an eye-witness account. The only
real atrocity seen so far by our boys was observed by Vernon
and Jack; they saw a National Guard shoot down a civilian
without provocation. These people are horrible, no one likes
them. They are merciless to prisoners. I jumped in on one
occasion and stopped them beating up a prisoner. Was I mad!

4.2.'45

A week, I know, but you will forgive and understand when I tell you I've been involved in getting *The Quadrant* going again. Issue No. 3 will be on the press in a couple of hours. We appear daily now, single sheet, and a double sheet on Sundays. This means a bigger staff; we now number sixteen, including a signaller with a super radio, and a Don-R, with a jeep in which for the last three days I have been bumping recklessly along much-pitted mountain passes to Athens, for news. We made the return journey the first night without lights, so that it is not surprising that we nearly pitched over a dangerously narrow bridge which we spotted only when we were two wheels over. Some of these roads are dizzy; towering mountain on your left hand, and a sickening drop to the right, below which are olive trees no bigger than button-holes.

The paper is still suffering birth pangs. A comp. has just come to report a snapped belt, while on the first night a vital casting snapped, limiting that issue to well below what it should have been. Because the paper is held in high esteem, R.E.M.E. were ordered to drop everything and get on with the breakage. They made a grand job of it. Second night the clutch failed, but very patiently Jack worked on, and the last copy was not so late after all. The machines remain temperamental, however, and when we eventually crawl into bed (we of the editorial room) it is always with the query: 'Will things go right with the machine tonight?' We are still mildly surprised when we find the papers to hand in the morning.

Yes, this is a country you haven't seen, and I should have a lot to say, but there is nevertheless a reluctance to say it, because I find a difficulty in saying it in an interesting manner, I believe. Then, too, my appetite has been satiated. I don't want new places and new sights; it's the old I hanker for. Oh! for that month's home leave!

We have eighteen on our staff now, three Scotsmen, an Irishman and a chap from Swansea. Then there is Antonio, a Greek cook. The cook is special because we keep crazy hours; some working by day, others by night, and a few overlapping. We have breakfast at eleven . . . it is now just after one in the morning, and if you aren't in bed you ought to be. At the moment I'm hanging on to read proofs coming in from the comps.

My growing reluctance to write is becoming an inability. I can't think of a thing here. Fortunately all we are doing is the news, and an occasional football match, as when, today, I reported a game at the Alexandros Stadium in Athens. These are easy enough. So long as nothing in any way creative is required. Today when the Greeks scored a goal—they were playing a famous Scottish regiment—showers of paper money were thrown in the air, in bundles probably representing a minor fortune in pre-war days, but worthless now. Fluttering down it made me think of a Broadway hero's homecoming. Mary would have loved the pipe-band that performed before the kick-off, and again during the interval.

Once I went to Khalkis to draw a Brigadier. A fierce Brigadier he was, with a bristling reputation, and bristling eyebrows.

You get to Khalkis from Thebes by the familiar mountain, twisting back so acutely and so often that were you a crocodile or an alligator (it really makes no difference) you'd have an awkward job not to tread on your own tail. You see Khalkis below you and a mountain-locked 'stadium' of water, blue and shining. You're bumping gently down to it, then you've lost it. You look around for it, and find it behind you, for the jeep has just turned round a precarious hairpin. The olives are below and for twenty miles you have been scattering goats and passing huge bundles of faggots which move along on four fragile and uncertain legs which belong, not to the kindling as you might suppose but to a little donkey who is hidden under its load. But now you've spiralled down and are on the flat, and approaching the bridge. It is guarded, since it connects Khalkis with the mainland. The guard, blancoed and standing to attention as the Brigadier's car goes by, never realizes that above the spot where he is standing Aristotle, in a desperate attempt to understand the tricky tides there, met his death by drowning. Neither did I until tonight when I read it in our own paper. But then perhaps the sentry knows that local legend is unreliable, and that in fact, he died in B.C. 322 after an illness. But Aristotle did study the tides here, after he had fled from Athens when threatened with persecution for impiety.

9.3.'45

With the fumes of cognac gently muzzing my head I'll endeavour to write you a *billet doux*. The company is deplorable, five compositors, one reader, and Willie the jeep driver. We've been working all out today and yesterday, sorting type which became mixed when the composition truck decided to lay down in a ditch.

The bar in which I write this is in a mediocre street. Opposite is a church, five years old, just unwrapped, so to speak, very clean and of a shape peculiar to all these Greek Orthodox Churches.

There is a square in front, and here it was that we all piled off the truck—to see a dancing bear! He was about five foot on his hind legs and had an awful lot of iron chain weighting the ring in his nose. Poor little bear. His, no doubt, was a lonely and miserable life. A crowd gathered round, and the owner banged his tambourine and pulled the chain round a stick, which made the bear follow his tender nose. The man's mate sawed at a sort of violin, bulbous at the back, like a spring onion split in half. He held it in front of him, by the neck as though it was a chicken; and now I come to think of it, the noise might have been an improvement had it been a chicken. When the music stopped, the owner thrust his tambourine under our noses, and we fished for a note and threw it in. Then they went away, the bear coming down on all fours and boys running behind trying to kick it.

But to get back to the bar. We were met with a scrumptious smell and a scrumptious sizzling sound—there at the counter, right by the door, a man was frying fish. We had some on a plate, done brown and breadcrumby. I could go for that stuff in a big way. But you never know how much they'll pile the price on. The room is spacious, with a dozen tables; no saloon and public division, but a sort of minstrel's gallery along the back. The bar, unlike most, has a wooden floor instead of the cold tiled one. A grey cat is coughing on one of the tables.

I've just stuffed a green envelope for you with cuttings from the paper. One is a story of a 'shipwreck'. The 'ship' was a Bailey bridge on floats, which the engineers were sailing through and around the islands on a five-day voyage. I am sure no sailor would ever have attempted the journey, but fools rush in . . . The thing all but sank twice. Towards the end they ventured only on the calmest waters. It was towed by a Greek *caique*—a cork of a craft that pitched all over the place. I met this *caique* at a point along the coast and it took me back to where the Bailey was, half a day's journey away, awaiting good weather. I was to get a story.

It was a lovely journey to that meeting place. We went in a jeep along the coast road, very bumpy as all roads are, but it wound and climbed, until the sea was way below. The waves juggled with the sun—azure, amidst gobbets of gold; on the mountain it was a-blowing, buds were popping, and prima-vera limbering up.

The donkeys, horses and dogs had never seen a car along those tracks before, and away they fled with the owner hang-ing on to them, the cargo—wood and wine—straining to fall off. All the goats spilled over the edge of the road, scuts bob-bing, and the dogs gave chase to us. A wonderful day with the air like wine. I couldn't help thinking of Jason and his *Argosy*, sailing round the islands. Then the road ended and even the jeep was stumped. We were at our rendezvous, a little village sprinkled along the bay. There were nets hung up to dry, slogans on the wall and a crowd drifting towards us. Sure enough, there was one in front who had been to the States. He greeted us with 'Howya, boys'. On the *caique*, nosing towards the Bailey, sitting alongside the tiller, was a Sgt. Webb from Truro. In the circumstances he wasn't feeling so far from home. There were three Greeks on board, the crew. On our right was a range of snow-topped mountains, the long white tail of Pegasus streaking to Helicon.

We went to the Bailey, which was moored in a creek. A few high-prowed ships, in process of being built, were strutted up below houses, built one above the other, higgledy-piggledy. Golden rock, white houses, blue sea gurgling; goats, black, white, vivid, going up the mountain, impossibly and at speed. The women wore long skirts in a full octave of colours. They were going up and down the rock like goats, carrying bundles balanced on their heads, with never a hand to steady them. There were barefoot children in boats, standing with two tiny hands working an oar, their reflections wriggling on the water.

There was no road through the village, only a path to slip and hop and balance upon, a stepping-stone path. I went along it to the pub later that night. The pub was dim, with salty fisher folk sitting around, drinking *retsina*. We nodded and sat down, bought the next table a drink and ate a small flat fish which was sharp with tiny bones, and flat as a leaf. The Cockneys sang 'All my Life I've Been a Barrow Boy'; the Scotsman took the high road and the low, until one Cockney slipped below the table and stayed there and the

Greeks thought—who knows what they thought. I wish I knew the language.

22.3.'45

There's another place I've got to bring you to. I've been ecstatic over lots of scenery, and I've seen a lot of marvellous stuff in that line, but yesterday we all climbed a mountain for two hours and saw scenery that beats everything so far.

While the snow is yet at the top, spring is busy in the gullies and on the slopes, and blossom bursts in unexpected places—a trill on the flute among the deeper sounds. One would have to mint a lot of new words, in gold, in colour, in music, before one could attempt to describe this. And oh! the lovely mountain villages, and the view when you look up, and back, and down. . . . A black-and-white burst below, and a magpie is gliding out, the sun on its wings. There's rushing water everywhere, spilling down the rocks with sounds of happiness. There's a tiny bridge over the ravine with here and there a thrust of cypresses, and sure enough a little church in the middle of them. All the rocks are a rich brown and green, and the roofs of staunch little houses below all made with that green rock which flakes easily, for tiling. And flowers, my love, bird's-eye and violets, daisies and marigolds and others. And little donkeys, three foot high, with impossible heads. Darlings! Behind one is the bay, pearly blue and all but lost in the shimmer of heat. Over there, sheep, like white maggots on a green cheese; a white horse, adult but thumbnail size on this canvas, near a gnarled Greek bending by the stream, deep, so deep in the gulley. He swings an axe, and the sound of it arrives half a minute late. But I can't describe it. *Kala nitka*, my love.

Yesterday I met tragedy, and couldn't find the cause, not being able to speak the language. A pig was lying on the side of the road. Its throat was cut as though an axe had been driven into it. I thought that they wouldn't kill it purposely, not on the road. Perhaps a passing army truck had struck it? Yet the cut was neat, and in the place the Greeks deal the death blow to animals. A little girl called something to me and it sounded angry as though she was calling shame on me. Was it the truck which did the damage? Then a lad came with a rope, made a kind of harness of it, fitted it round the pig, then a woman hauled it towards Stilis. Thirty yards along another little girl with her head in her arms was leaning against an olive tree, sobbing bitterly. Within an orchard was a woman milking a goat. She passed her hand across her eyes and I saw that she was weeping, too. There was a sow tied to the tree by her side. I couldn't understand it. Were they weeping for the pig? Had the two scenes any connection? I was helpless without language, and could only stand and watch sympathetically.

23.4.'45

Stilis cemetery is a small cemetery, with a squat church and lines of tapering cypresses. The grass is tall and thronged with ragwort, daisies and poppies. They riot, as the expression is, they riot like the bones. And it's the bones that make this story a gruesome one. There are bones in baskets, bones in boxes and bones in bags. Bones everywhere. Human bones.

They make you shudder. The custom decrees that a person shall be dis-interred after three years. Or what is left of him/her. (The language needs another personal pronoun.) Normally the bones then go in a box. Nowadays it seems no boxes are used at Stilis. Whether through shortage of wood or because the Germans declared the cemetery *verboten*, I don't know. But the place is slipping into a queer reversal of status, and if no check is made, instead of burying it will itself be buried.

All along the enclosing wall of the cemetery bones gleam in the grass, and on scores of graves they are piled in pyramids. In the middle of one pile is a photograph: the external appearance of the flesh the bones once supported. In this case a middle-aged man with a proud moustache. In the corner of the cemetery is a little stone building. The grass outside is littered with bones, and heaped into the angle of the wall are some twenty skulls and hundreds of ribs and lesser bones. As I looked at them a spider scuttled across a skull and on a shiny strand of silk descended into the cavity where once a lively eye had been.

I went up six stone steps and looked into the building. It was a warehouse of bones. Many were in wooden chests with names and crosses painted on them. There were fully a hundred of such boxes, some bursting open. But not all the bones had such storage. Some swung in bags from the rafters where the spiders were, and some were piled on bits of rusty tin. Somebody had scooped them up as you would ashes from a fire, and with a grim sense of decoration had wedged the skull firmly on top. I didn't venture inside because the floor was rotten, and I could see more bones in the cellar below; besides I was feeling nausea by now. Outside, it was possible to see into the cellar by a grating, tibulas, fibulas, femurs, patellas and pelvic bones, scapulas, clavicles, ribs and hundreds of skulls filled the room from floor to ceiling. Who were they, or who had they been? Man, woman, laughing child, lovely girl, fisherman, thief, rich, poor. Well, you can't take it with you, and here they were all together in a charnel house. All in all the finest argument for cremation possible.

Two Greeks whom I asked about this practice left nothing decided. It is a religious custom, they said. Then one told me that the graves were leased for three years. When the lease expires they are given notice to quit. But you may extend the lease if you wish, and may buy the land permanently if you like. But all the bones are put in boxes, I was assured. The bones in Stilis might be so mixed because the Germans shot many hostages against the cemetery walls and buried them in common graves. If this is the story behind the bones it is indeed a terrible indictment, but after a while and a little thought the Greek said: 'There are poor folk who go into common graves, too.' Any dead wheeled to the burial ground in a cart and left there—apparently this is not uncommon—go into the common graves.

Mike, the interpreter of the Field Security Police, told me some more graveyard customs. Three days after burial the relatives go to the graveside with a sort of porridge, containing sugar and currants. They sprinkle some on the grave, and the rest they eat themselves. The wheat signifies ripeness, according to Mike, and the other ingredients sweetness—a full and sweet life. Later the process is repeated, and performed again when the bones are dug up after the expiral of the lease. When the bones come up they are allowed to bleach in the sun, and then are bathed in red wine—the blood of Jesus—either

M
177

Samos or Mavrodaphne. Then into a box, and periodically looked to. He has seen a relative kiss a skull before now. This whole practice, however, is beginning to dwindle and is not carried out in Athens; though in a suburb of that city, we passed through a cemetery and saw bones stored in boxes there.

In the islands they have all sorts of queer customs. One is the employment of professional mourners, not only at the burial but periodically afterwards. They wail, gnash teeth and rend their hair. The payment is in kind, eggs, wine and so on.

No, I won't ask you to share my dottiness for birds, but the other day I saw no fewer than twenty-seven eagles in the air all at once. They circled round for ten minutes with never a wing beat between them, catching the air currents in their magnificent wings all the time. The kids here are deadly with catapults. One hit a hawk the other day, I could have brained him. I brought it to the billet, but the wound was in the head and it died after a time. It was a lovely thing. I drew it, but I'd have loved to have been able to keep it for a pet.

Kala nikta.

4.5.'45

Today, a month after ours, is the Greek Good Friday. The people are fasting, eating no meat or oily foods—just bread, and I believe potatoes are permitted. I have just been out to see a procession. It is a warm night with big stars and the day has been marked by Greek flags all at half-mast, and the tolling of bells from a half-dozen churches. The solemnity of one tolling nearby floats through the window now. A dismal sound, the tolling of a single bell. The procession was led by

GREECE, 1944-5

white-robed boys carrying candles, and a bigger boy holding aloft a garlanded cross of wood. Behind him came the men, a dozen in a bunch, singing harmoniously. More children bore suns and stars, brass insignia of the Greek Orthodox Church mounted on varnished poles which gave an occasional glinting response to the candlelight. Then came two patriarchs of the Church, chimney-pot hats, venerable beards and long, long trappings. Both carried brass-bound Bibles, holding them open and pressed to their august bosoms. The procession moved slowly, hanging a long time on each foot. The centre piece was in the shape of a bier as I supposed it to be. This was borne by four of the procession on their shoulders and was closely bound with flowers. Old men and women and many children were in the procession, chatting and laughing in spite of the solemnity of the occasion. All carried little candles sheltered by their hands, and each threw a light on the face of the holder. It was good fun for the kids. As the retinue moved slowly along candles appeared at doors and balconies all along the street. On some balconies they were arranged in a row along the top of the ironwork. The whole thing was very pretty and with the slow ring of the bells, quite impressive.

6.5.'45

The servant woman, who has a kindly smile and goes about her work in bare feet, shook my hand this morning and said 'Krista Nesta'. The lady of the house, who shows gold teeth with every smile of her fat face, gave me a red egg, a little cake, and a glass of *ouzo*. It is the Greek Easter. I told you about the candlelight procession in my last letter. Today Christ is risen and shots go off all around, many lambs turn

179

on spits, and Greeks tuck in to repair the period of fast. The coloured eggs often have the words 'Christ is risen' written on them, the priests having announced it the previous midnight.

It is the custom for two people to bang their eggs together, the one whose egg cracks last being assured of good luck. Paul, our Greek cook, and the pleasant little bedraggled woman who helps him with the washing-up, both observed the fast in spite of cooking more or less sybarite dishes for us. And this morning one of my 'family' called bringing her little brother with her, he having had a skin-tight haircut. She smiled shyly, showing her little white teeth and the gaps between them. She was clean for the first time since she introduced herself about a month ago, and her face looked a little bit rosier than usual from scrubbing. She asked me for a caramella; it is purely a commercial arrangement, you see, this visiting. She waited by the gate and I went in and returned with a bar of chocolate. She said 'efharisto', and holding her brother by the hand retreated slowly backwards, smiling shyly all the time, till the polite distance having been covered she turned her back on me and began tearing off the wrapping, both heads close together over it. Pretty. On most occasions she and her friends ask for 'farina'—bread. It betrays a desperate past when a child asks for bread before sweets. A loaf must have been a very Eldorado a month ago.

V.E. Day

Dear Spouse,

Today is V.E. Day. I wonder how, and if, you are celebrating it. We heard Churchill's speech, scribbling rapidly to get it *verbatim* for tonight's edition. We didn't succeed. Later we

tried to get some of the scenes in London from the broadcast
from street microphones. It had little effect on this town,
though the bells were ringing this afternoon when I went out
to see if anything was doing. The town was dozing just the
same as ever, indoors and out of the hot dusty streets. Last
night a party was held to try and infuse some life into the
proceedings. I had to sing 'Sweet Chariot' as I always have to,
but was all agin' it. I wanted to lie in the fields and look at
the stars and think, and perhaps cry. I felt in a funny mood
and at odd moments all through the day I'd think of young
Hilda. For the hundreds of kids just like her today it must
have been just hell. No, I didn't care for celebrating.

We've heard the King's speech, four scribbling furiously
and sweating at the finish. Then we compared notes and though
we can sometimes read what we have got down, we can never
piece the thing completely together. There always seem to be
gaps. We were round the comps.' truck till a late hour. It was
a warm night full of little flying insects, and now and then the
sound of storks rattling their beaks.

Today I was sitting typing in this room, the sun blazing
away outside and we in our shorts again, when the door
opened and a boy of about nine said: 'Mister, mister,' and
gave me a piece of cardboard on which was pencilled the
following note:

> *Friends, English soldiers us young boys seven of us*
> *we have a little automobile and we wish to go to*
> *Stylis at sea-coast to take bath, but we have no petrole*
> *or benzine. Will you please give us two (2) gallons*
> *of petrole for our automobile and we will appreciated—*
> *the Seven Kids-John-Telis-Nick-Philo-John-Stefos.*

He had big eyes and a shaven head this kid, and the rest of the variety act had shaven heads too. But there was no sign of an automobile at the gate, and it might have been a gag. In any case we can't give away petrol. 'English *lago* petrol,' I said—that's little or small—'English *polli* petrol,' he replied. They could bath here easily with the many street pumps about, but it was a swim they wanted more than anything.

11.5.'45

Glad you've heard from Mary. I was wondering about her the other day. Pleased to know that Alec's home, and couldn't agree more with Mary's comment that it's time we were too. Over two years. No one seems to realize just what that means. We've got a fellow here who's had four years of it, all through the desert and still at it. He'a nice looking Aberdonian, ginger and O.K. when he's off the drink, but the four years have ruined him and he drinks and has drunk so much that he's all of a tremble. Should be sent home on medical grounds anyway.

But I doubt if he'll ever fully recover, but can you blame him for drinking, four years of loneliness? He's quite young, too. He has one good restraining influence in a girl he's sweet on in Athens, with the lovely name of Leah. When the boys go to Athens, on leave or in the course of their jobs, they all stay at her place. She's a very intelligent girl, speaking about four languages. She knows us all and wants to know when I am going down, so I am told. I don't think I shall because I don't want to go there for my leave and I always refuse to go there on business. Still, Leah sounds so solicitous that . . . But I tease you, please be jealous.

This letter is making hard writing. I feel awful tonight. Can't settle down to anything, but there's an odd turn of thought from Ernest lying on his bed behind me. He's been counting *drachmae*, and suddenly mumbles at me through his moustache—which fine-toothcombs his speech to nigh inaudibility—that if you were long-lived and you had put one *drachmae* in the bank every year since A.D.1 'You'd have quite a lot to draw, now wouldn't you?' To which I said: 'Yes, I would.' And Ernest said: 'Well, you wouldn't, you'd have £3 4s. 10d.' And so you would. I asked him the why for of such an odd train of thought and he said he had just counted 1,950 *drachmae* and had thought to himself: 'Oh, dear, I hope I don't have to wait to 1950 to go home.' It's the main thought you see. And it has been for years and years.

30.5.'45

You haven't heard from me for over a week, on account of my being deaf. I went swimming and my colossal ears drained the Aegean, several vessels being left high and dry on their keels. Quite an interesting sight actually, ships careened to the right and to the left, captains megaphoning from the bridges and whistles tootooing full blast, but still none of them able to move an inch. Every time I moved my head cubic fathoms swished round and round it. When the moon rose it drew the tide over to my right ear. I couldn't sleep after that, I never knew earache could be so painful. I paced up and down till dawn and it didn't go off then, so I went sick. They found I had a temperature of 101 and put me in a marquee as Fever (N.Y.D.) not yet diagnosed. I was kept there three days. One night you would have thought there was a wild

183

cat in my mosquito net. That was me dealing with a Grecian spider—two inches long—before he dealt with me. Then I came down by road—you have to see these roads to know what that meant—to No. 72 General Hospital at Athens, where I am now. The ear still aches slightly and makes listening a strain. However, I am in good company. Scruff Barton was here, Stan and several others. They all went down with a sort of pneumonia. Not so severe as the type we know, but more prevalent.

1.6.'45

I find it hard to forgive another week's abstinence from writing. Spring cleaning! I snort. What is it but chucking out things that should be kept, and a high-handed purging of carefully collected reference cuttings? I have always found it so, and lost a hundred drawings yearly that way, so that I spat at the primrose and scowled at the cuckoo. I forbid it in our house, FORBID it, understand. That's Lord Gunn, and meaning it!

My ear but marks time. I now get penicillin. A twenty-four-hour course yesterday, followed by a repeat dose today. I'll be mighty glad when it ends, and have thought some hard things about Alexander Fleming, for every injection is made in my buttock with the added indignity of a charming sister to perform the job. Every three hours I have an injection of 15,000 units. That is about the equivalent of a tuppeny bottle of castor oil in quantity. It is vaseline colour, and so far I've had ten jabs, all on the same side, which, believe me, suffers me not to sit thereon. I'm up. One can distinguish the penicillin patients by reason of their one-sided stance at the tables.

But the third hour approaches. Oh dear!—I feel like one of those sacks they hang up for bayonet practice. 'Please, sister, don't charge this time,' I besought. 'Make a standing lunge.' She'll be tripping in soon with that tray, wadding, iodine, the penicillin (I'm full of it) and that glass syringe with the long, long needle.

The hospital here is good, and of a fair size. The foyer of the main entrance is distinguished by a large heroic portrait of Hitler on the wall, quite well done, but as it's a mural, hard to remove. They have contented themselves with gouging the eyes and obliterating the moustache. Above the stage of the concert hall stretches the black blotch of the Nazi Eagle.

20.6.'45

If you have eyes to see you can see, I said, and if you are any good at all you can fill a letter. So at eight o'clock, when I left the disorder of the billet to go round to breakfast, I went down the small flight of stone steps, paused at the gateway, and looked around. There, over the road, on both the right side and the left, were the storks, the bulky nest damming the gutters and three youngsters standing up in one, half as tall as mother already. What an array of spindly shanks! All four beaks were held open, agape as a dog's is when it pants from the heat. 'Good morning, storks,' I said, but though I said it very affable-like, they ignored me and just went on gaping. This is a characteristic pose. The beak is held thus so that they can begin their machine-gun rattling—a peculiar sound that goes on and off all through the day and night—at split-second notice. The youngsters looked around, up and down at the pavement. 'When are you going to teach us to fly,

Mum?' One of them apparently tried it the other day. I'm
told he fell off the roof all ways but before he could hit the
deck, a matter of ten feet below because their particular nest
is on a bungalow, one of the parent birds had swooped and
caught him. I don't know how, whether in claws, on back, or
beak, but it is a surprising feat for a creature of such leisurely
movement. The old man was away in the rushes of the plain,
I should say, looking for frogs. He'd be back soon, no doubt
—an arrow-like zip through the air with the long beak thrust-
ing like a spear, a braking action with his huge wings; and
with a comical dangling of legs he'd be alighting with the
breakfast. Meanwhile, what of mine? So I left the four of
them standing monumentally in their untidy circle of twigs
and wondering how they stuck up there all day in this merciless sun, which is making me sweat already. The storks in the
other nest were more cautious; none of their heads showed
above the level of the nest.

Along the street I went, turning right then left into the road
where lately market stalls have appeared—having been evicted
from the square below. The shadows hung on the wall like
curtains. A woman came along leading a pony. The pony was
laden with twigs. I don't like that practice, for the twigs are
sharp and the animal has no adequate covering. I have seen
a dozen all alongside one another in the market place, and
every one had blood trickling from numerous cuts. The
woman had a bundle of faggots on her back too, and she
was short and stocky and purposeful, extending the pony's
head on the rope with which she led it.

There were stalls along the road, full of varied wares, including a great deal of stuff originating from quartermasters'
stores. Courts-martial for selling army kit have been a fre-

quent occurrence. Women, ragged, scarves over heads, preside over an array of vegetables; beans, marrows, peas, most of it an unhealthy yellow-seared colour, too rapidly forced by this driving climate.

There are peaches, too, but these aren't very appetizing, either. The prices are still high for Greeks, but a new currency arrangement applicable only to the army has brought stuff into our range that was formerly well out of it. Two ragged barefooted boys wrestle on the pavement and a little girl and a man eat fish—sprat-sized—from the same plate on the kerb, in the shade of a lovely tree which covers the open-fronted baker's shop here very effectively, and makes an interesting picture.

I don't know whether it's a plague, or a regular thing at this time of the year, but the place is full of flying crickets, almost as numerous as flies, and more revolting. When their wings are open they show a salmon-coloured body, and they might be bits of apple-blossom with two trailing legs. The fields were never free of them most all the way from Athens, and now and then one would sail in at the side of the jeep and strike you forcibly in the face and worse still, sometimes drop into your shirt.

Well, I got my breakfast, but what was the good? I ate only one slice and a bit of bacon. It's always like that; I haven't been able to eat a big meal for years. Mebbe your culinary prowess will change all that.

26.6.'45

Dear Wife,

My ears are now better, I have been swimming three times but didn't stay in long because they began to threaten. Guess I'll have to use your swimming hat when I get home. When I get home! Now I am back with the unit.

Found this on the wall of a restaurant in Lamia, still Greek to us.

COMPLET MENY

EGGSS AND CHIPS

LIVER AND ONIOS

PORK CHAPS

FRITE FICH

RETSINA

WIN MAYRODAFRI

Greeks are famous for their wrestling so we expected to see some good things last Sunday when contests were held here. We didn't. First disappointment was the ring, which wasn't a ring at all, nor set centrally, but an uneven palliasse placed on the rickety stage of the Open Air Theatre. The National Guard, with rifles and bandoliers, gave the thing a good build up. Looked like there would be plenty of *berlud*. Even the timekeeper had a rifle across his table. The first fight was a tame draw, but as the contestants had been seen together on the Square, and were obviously good friends, this was not surprising. Fight number two promised well. A six-year feud existed between the maulers, and from the way they glowered at each other, it looked it. Moreover it was all-in. In Greek all-in, however, one must not club one's man with a stool, gouge his eyes, or tie the ref. in a sheet-bend as in the honest-to-goodness British. The extra freedom is restricted to punching in the back of the neck, twisting the foot, and wobbling your opponent's nose with the palm of your hand. Kittenish stuff! A generous lubrication of sweat enabled the smaller man to eel-out of many holds, but just as we were reconciled to another draw he found one hold too much for him, and yelled submission. That, we found, was the finish of the show —a lousy hundred *drachmas* worth. Perhaps the winner felt this, too, and that may have decided him to sing. Anyway, no one had the temerity to say such a muscle-bound brute nay, and he sang. It was a wailing song, showing strong Turkish influence, and had the effect of making me wish heartily that the other man had won.

Good night,

ROBBIE.

Infantry Record Office,
ASHFORD, *Middlesex*.
24th July 1945.

Madam,

It is my painful duty to inform you that a report has been received from the War Office notifying the death of:
(No.) 6350810   (RANK) LANCE-CORPORAL
(NAME) Walter Stanley ROBSON,
(REGIMENT) The Queen's Own Royal West Kent Regiment which occurred in Greece
on the 13th July 1945.

Lt.-Col. H. P. Braithwaite,
1 R.W.K.,
C.M.F.,
17th July 1945.

Dear Mrs. Robson,

It is with a very sad heart that I am writing to convey to you my deepest sympathy in your great loss. The death of your husband came as an awful shock to us all as I fear it will have done to you. As I am sure you must realize 'Robbie' as he was affectionately known by all, was a very prominent and popular personality in the battalion. In action he was fearless and always put the care and needs of his fellow soldiers before himself. Out of action, he always took an active interest in any doings of the battalion and one of his greatest and most praiseworthy achievements was his work in organizing and running our Battalion Casualty Fund, which has helped at least in a small way numerous wives and children of those great men who have given their lives for us.

We in this battalion have indeed lost a great soldier and a great gentleman and I would like to express to you on behalf of the whole battalion our gratitude for your husband's excellent work and comradeship and to convey to you our very deepest sympathy in your bereavement.

Yours sincerely,

PERCY BRAITHWAITE.

Postscript

I have offered the letters of my husband for publication partly because he himself had hoped to write some account of his experiences when he returned, and this was the only way in which I could carry out that wish, and partly because I thought that there was room for a war book which was not written around some exciting incident or escape, but showed war as it really was from the point of view of the ordinary front-line soldier.

There is a reason for the gap between the last letter and the letter from the Record Office. There were a few letters after the one dated June 26th. My husband was ill for about ten days before he died, of what his friends thought was heat stroke. He was unable to write, and they did not write, thinking that such letters would alarm me unnecessarily. However, he was more seriously ill than they thought. He died, according to the official certificate, of 'Acute caseating Pulmonary Tuberculosis and heat stroke'.

One point remains to be cleared up. Some of the letters are addressed to Margaret Gunn. This was one of his nicknames for me. Having been stationed for a while in Scotland he had become 'more Scotch than the Scots', and apparently the Robsons belong to the Gunn clan.

I am grateful to Mr. Williamson for editing and writing an Introduction to these letters of the most gentle, modest, and kindly person I have ever met.

MARGARET ROBSON.